Mai-Mai (Somali) DICTIONARY

Mai-Mai to English

Seqend Hussain

Copyright © 2018 by Seqend Hussain.

All rights reserved. No part of this publication may be reproduced, distributed, or transmitted in any form or by any means, including photocopying, recording, or other electronic or mechanical methods, without the prior written permission of the author, except in the case of brief quotations embodied in critical reviews and certain other noncommercial uses permitted by copyright law.

Printed in the United States of America.

ISBN	Paperback	978-1-948653-08-4
	Hardback	978-1-948653-09-1
	eBook	978-1-948653-10-7

Authors Press
California, USA

www.authorspress.com

A

aa used to confirm understanding

aabyh *lexicon* "father"

aabo *lexicon* person's father

aamiy *transitive verb* ate

aamow eater

aamey or **aantoy** *feminine* eater

aanq or **aam** eat

aama *plural* eat

aanq-aanq *noun* something to eat

aanqto food or something to eat

aar vengeance, revenge

aaran spring season

aario air

aari to put air in, pump

aaria *plural* to put air in, pump

aaruri to pick up (things) on floor or on ground, gather

aasami to thank

aasan favour, mercy

aasanqo preferably, rather than

aasantei thanks

aascuas to put (something) together or to plan to

aasi disobedient, bad child

aathi normal, cool, okay

aaw father

Aaw' Malan Father's Day

Aaw'o fathers, the fathers

aawko siblings who have same father, but not same mother

aay mother

Aay' Malan Mother's Day

Aay'o mothers, the mothers

aayow person's mother

aayow hoy an expression; "Hey, Mother!" or "Oh, Mother!"

aay yar aunt from mother side

aaywasse motherfucker

aaytzo siblings who have same mother, but not same father

aba self, selves

abaay sweety (female)

abasheh itself

abay elder sister

abay yal elder sisters

abaay or **abaayo** a term of endearment for "sweetheart"

abayow a person's elder sister

abayed a full-length loose-fitting robe worn by Muslim women (*abaya*)

abay kalled another elder sister

abbareeg teapot

abbareeg'o the teapots

Abdi male name; servant of God

Abdullahi male name; servant of God

Abduraman male name; servant of God

Abduramani variant of *Abdi*

abbitan beverage

abir to measure

abiris tape measure

abitey kite

abobou elder brother

aboo sweety (male)

abosto great

abou elder brother

abou kalled another elder brother

abul nest

abul shimbir bird nest

abul shinni bee hive

address address

adh white colour

adhdan white person

adhdai to make (something) white

adhdenq proof

adhdeay prove

addonq slave

addon feminine of *addonq*

addomey slavery

af mouth, language

afbilaw breakfast

afbilaw aanq eat breakfast

afbilawo have breakfast

afdaibble dragon

affar four; tetra

affarayd forth

affar bogol four hundred

affar dhini four side

affargais quadrilateral

affar gour four time

affar jair four time

affar marr four time

affartan forty; 40

afartan bogol forty hundred; four thousand

afartan kun forty thousand

affartan milyon forty million

affurr the first meal of the day for a fasting person; after sunset meal (*iftar*)

afimad wellness, health

afkazhe brunch

afkazheay have brunch

aflagada profanity

aflawb snack

afoqadto avocados

afteen light, shine

afteeni to flash on

afuf to blow with mouth

affaara business, personal business

aeg near, side

agaar green

agal material, stuff

agg wheel or tire

aggkuras or **garikuras** wheelchair

Ahad Sunday

ahan instance, like, for

aharo any, to be

ahato *feminine* any, to be

ahaw to be or accept in giving

ahay past tense of *is* and *are*

ahayniy were (used with "we")

ahayena were (used with "they")

ahayiy was, it was

Ahmad male name; most praised

ai somebody must, supposed do

aidhiss AIDS

aidi to turn toward to, face to, direct to

aido stepmother

aiffi forgive

aih will

Aisha female name; living or womanly

aimis insurance

airaid back, the rear part of body

airain goat

airain yal goats

airaindajiow shepherd; goatherd; herdsman

airaineelaley sheep

airaingandol or **airaingandola** fatty sheep; sheep

ais grass

aisin niece

aisinq nephew

aithaib manners, discipline

aithan a call for prayers, to make prayer calls

ajal cassette

ajal rathiou radio cassette or music cassette

ajal philink video cassette

ajarr thigh

ajarr a good deed point from God

ajarr hasanat good deed from God

ajiin dough

ajis idle; lazy

ajislima shiftless

ajissole a lazy person

ajusa an old lady who has teenage spirit

akbaar a while

akd by, toward, near, way, at

ala *verbal auxiliary* may

al somebody has to do (something) about (something)

alab tableware; dishes

alacx expression of lie

alad instrument

alaikum (*Arabic*) upon you

alhamdulillah (*Arabic*) thank God; praise belongs to Allah

allamenda exercise, work out

allanji masticate

alan flag

alen tea

alen agaar green tea

alen qharer bitter tea

aligorop a plant that has long thorns everywhere

allaf fortune

allamo mark

allamo'o the marks

allamoy to trace, mark

alol belly

alqaptar helicopter

alwah wood

alwah yal woods

amalle maybe (used at the beginning of sentence)

amamiso itchiness

amamizhoye itching

amamio poison ivy

amar order, command

amauh borrow, lend

ambeo or

ambea mango

ameer prince

ameerad princess

amoor getting-together party that involves food

ambpira rubber

ambulo boiled corn kernels or boiled beans and corn kernels

ameen amen

Amina a female name; trustworthy

amin trust

amin lauag trust fund

ambalas ambulance

amal same as, as

amus *lexicon* "quiet"

anab grape

anano to teach manners

andin fleshy, fat

andun world

andunyo earth

ann don't (used to refer to other people or things)

ani I am, I

ani ei moudti let me pass

anigu *lexicon* "I" or "me"

anjera a round flat soft Somali bread that is made of flour and cornmeal

anjhal chew

anjhara dove

anjhara biyo water dove; forest dove

anjhara buured brown-feather dove, morning dove

anjhara goondo pigeon

anjhara maar red- or copper-eyed dove

anjhara mazhow black-eyed dove; water dove

Anjhairey a little tiny bird that has a small sharp beak

anne are, it is, is (used with *we* or *us*)

anqshag to like

anqshagiy liked, like

anqfa benefit

ansalatto salad

ansha ethic

anshab full handed of (something)

anshoor tax

anyawo a form of entertainer for festival purpose

aoodubillah (Arabic) "May God protect me from evil. I seek refuge with Allah."

apshir thanks god; hallelujah

apsi fear

apso afraid

apti maternal uncle

aptiow person's maternal uncle

aqar final, finale

aqara afterlife

aqbal agree

aqbaliy agreed

aqbar report

aqlag character

aqli smartness, intellect

aqligal logic

aqtar actor

aqtarisha actress, heroine

aqtora the good guy in movie, hero, protagonist

aqliste alcoholic

aqri read, recite

aqriqar readable

aqye due, to end

aqte *feminine* due, to end

aqyaar an adult male person that settles or appraises marriage dowry; very mature male

Arab Arab

Arab'o the Arabs

Arafah the twelfth month

arag to see

aragiy saw

araja a sloppy or messy person

araro to complain or issue problem so can be fix

arauaro spider

Arbah Wednesday

Arbay female name; guardian

arday student

arday yal students

arewa slob; sloppy

ararr *lexicon* "run"

argois crab

ariir *lexicon* "child"

ariri to make (a place) crowded

aririy crowded, tight

armajo cabinet

armal widow

aros marry, wedding

arosiy married

arosi to get (someone) married

arr to dare not to do (something)

arraf fragrance

arra sands

arrap tongue

arra waar beach sand

arsanya lobster

arsany yal lobsters

aryn convocation, issue, case

asahab group, gang

asan scarlet

asbauh misbegotten

Asha variant of *Aisha*; living

ashcuash to feel disgusted

ashauarrapdhear rainbow

ashar assignment, lesson

ashe dinner

asheay have dinner

ashe aanq eat dinner

ashita acid

ashun water pot

ashun yal water pots

ashur duty

Asneen Monday

asqar police

assalamu alaikum (*Arabic*) a salutation: peace be upon you

assar afternoon, afternoon prayer

assarcui to be obvious or having connection toward the prayer of afternoon

astarre enjoy

astur put in save

athab *intransitive verb* torture

athal fair

athaig shopping, errand

athaigiy past of *athaig*

athair stepfather or paternal uncle

athaihg very hard

atheay to brush

atheayso to brush (teeth)

athi you

athigu *lexicon* "you"

ato skinny

attang are, it is (used with "you guys")

atte are

attena *plural* are (used only with *you guys*)

Auw Mr. (usually used with a name)

Auw Usman the seventh month

Auy Ms., Mrs. (usually used with a name)

awaad complain

awaal award

awaalguzhd or **awaalmarin** reward, prize

awaar recession, famine, drought

awghon orphan

awesa big snake

awoor to plant, to plant seed

awoor bouor pumpkin seed

awoor hashish cannabis seed

awoor sisin sesame seed

awoa grandfather

awoa yal grandfathers

awor termite

awor'o the termites

awor yal termites

awoud power, ability to do something

awoy grandmother

awoygudey grasshopper

awurey dune lizard

awuro fence lizard

awud worship

ayahd a verse in Quran

ayaan name of day

ayeyow person's nana

ayey nana

Ayoob or **Ayub** male name; patience and devout; one of the prophet's name

ayow an expression; "please"

ayowcuayow an expression; "oh my gosh"

ayuu to give an evil eyes or curse

ayuunq *adjective* the curse of jealousy or evil eyes

ayuunqminasi *noun* the curse of evil eyes or jealous eyes

ayyang are, it is (used with "they" or "them")

ayye I am, am, is

ayyena are, it is (used with *they* or *them*)

azhak to be hard on someone or Something

azhd *lexicon* "go"

Aziz male name; wise

B

ba dad, pa

baabyhi to ruin or destroy

baahi hunger

baahin need

baal feather

baal page

baal'o the pages

baalashuto parachute

baaldi bucket

baaleybaroro butterfly

baani to get spoil with food

baar to check, inspect

baare or **baarow** inspector

baari obedient child, good child

baariy past tense of *baar*

baartiy *feminine* past tense of *baar*

baas a Somali word for wagon animals; stop

baati a full-length loose-fitting cloak worn by some Muslim or Somali women

baathi protect

bauhrr when a something is past its due; expire

bauhrri to make (something) expire

bauhrriy expired

bauhrrtiy *feminine* expired

babbis hand fan

baba daddy; papa

babai papaya

babur vehicle

babur monq truck or big vehicle

bachag soft, chick: girl

bacgizhiy delayed

baddbaathie hero

baddbaathi to save; protect

baddbazhi boil

baddbazhihiy boiled

badd sea

baddfrais seahorse

baddfrais'o the seahorses

baddjiro seasick

baddoroni boss

bagg to be scare

bah go or leave

bahal Wight, creature

bahiy past tense of *bah*

bahtiy *feminine* past tense of bah

bahar difficult or risky situation

bahattin lump

bahr teach

bahre teacher

bahr use, to get used to (something)

bahro learn

bahrarow learner

bahriy taught

bahrtiy *feminine* taught

bahrow *female* teacher

baimbais ash

baimbaissaaranq ashtray

baiddail change

bailaidd city

bairr large amount; some

bairri tomorrow

bairridambe the day after tomorrow

bairridambe bairrishe the day after the day after tomorrow

bairobairou not straight to any direction

bais enough; no more

bacji to delay

bakayle rabbit

bakhar warehouse

bakkairi mug; cup

bakkairi yal plural of **bakkairi**

bakkuli bowl

bakkuli yal bowls

bakkin parking lot

bal dracaena: corn plant or any treelike tropical plant of the genus

balan appointment, agreement, promise, deal

ballanq aardvark

balle female rabbit

balug when a child reach puberty

balugiy past tense of *balug*

balugtiy *feminine* past of tense of *balug*

bamia okra

bambele grapefruit

banam blank

banaan vacancy

bandar jurisdiction safe area

bandera border

baniqol film; camera rolls

banjar flat

bannanq out, flat land

bannaw space

bannai to make space

banzin petrol

baos jail

baqag parrot

Baqar male name; inevitable

baqqoro walking cane

baqshad envelope

baradha potato

baraf ice, snow

baraf lefto ice cream

barafoye icing

baraful icicle

baraka blessings

baraka Allah (*Arabic*) "May God's blessings be on you."

barambara cockroach

barbaroni green pepper

bararr swell

bararriy swollen; swelled

barbaar a male teenager

bariima from beginning, first, before

bari sleep over

baryiy past tense of *bari*

baritiy *feminine* past tense of bari

barizd rice

barizd monqmonq Arborio rice

barnamij program

barxhin pillow

barqinjinni mushroom

barr trace, print, spot, dot, track, half

barrsad leopard

barroo swell: increase in number

barroowiy past tense of *barroo*

barsa living room

barud firecracker

baruji smash, crush

barur thick fat

barwaq bounty, plenty

barwaqo bountiful, plentiful

barye *lexicon* "beg"

basbaas chili pepper

bashal have good time, good time

bashal kee the good time

bashbash variant of *peace,* winter

baskiil bicycle

baskiil'o the bicycles

bassal onion

bass pass

bassabor passport

basta pasta

bastabibilar linguine

bastorr pistol

bastorr'o the pistols

batatagaid cassava

batata dhuled sweet potato

batata dhuled ground potato; the more it grows, the more it spreads on the ground

battaria battery

battaria'o the batteries

bazhan a lot, poly, lots

bazhazhiy became a lot

bazhi to make (something) into a lot

bazhi to gain a lot, win

bathiil shovel

baua plastic bag

bauan guilt

bauante guilty

bauanye *masculine* guilty

bauaw illegitimate, spurious

bauh used to express emotion

bauyd thick sand or beach sand

bazhul orange color

bazook bazooka

bcuar invest or to invest

bcue price

beaili waste

beeb flat can

behl pail

behr farm, garden

behr'o the farms, gardens

beala good

bele sans; less; not

bengi bank

benn lie, false

bennole liar

bennoley *female* liar

bennolow *male* liar

benn tzee the lie

benn wa it is false

ber liver

ber yal lives

ber yal kee the livers

ber'o the livers

besa money

bettiwinq vitamin

beuhr depend, rely

beyshin tub, bathtub

beyli free

beyligad a person who looks for free stuff

beyrkou unspecific number, some

bidd vanish

bidzha left

bibihiso act of taking (somethings) repeatly

bih to take (something) out, afford

bihi take (something) out

bihiso to take (something) out and keep it

bil moon, month

bilale gangster

bilamed feminine

bilan female

bilan sahib female friend

bilar broad, big and flat

bilash naught, free

bilashow free

bilaw start, begin

bilayo trouble

bilayole trouble maker

bilig flash

bill bill

biligbilig lighting

bilyon billion

bilyon kun billion thousand`

biin safety pin

biin'o the pins

binna adyn human being

binsa plier

bir steel; metal

bir anjhera solid and flat griddle pan

birpol pole

bir'o the metals

birdaiy mirror

birrbirr glow

bir jiir mouse trap

birri booty, buttock

bisad pussy cat

Bismillah (*Arabic*) God's will; in the name of Allah

biyo *plural* water

bastorr biyo water gun

biyo dhi water fall

biyo farrdiir warm water

biyo kawoub cold water

biyo kulel hot water

biyo qarrqarr very hot water

biyo saafi clear water, clean water

biyo dhusug dirty water

bizhar bald

biyq coward

biyqar virgin

biyr move or turn

bloun ball

bloun'o the balls

blouni splash ball; splash balloon

blubb pink

boab elope

boawiy past of boab

bogg cave, hole, an open hole

boggiy torn or got hold

boggsinye got hold

boggtiy *feminine* torn or got hold

bohs spot

bokkbougle esophagus

bokkis box

bokkis'o the boxes

bogol hundred

bogol kun hundred thousand

bogol milyon hundred million

bogor king

bogorad queen

bol bolt

bolombol mannequin

bolog district

bombal doll

bomba bomb

bonq a person that is soulless and selfish

boofi spray, pump

boofunq balloon

boos dent: crash trace

boosi to make (something) to have a dent

boosiy dented

boondo bridge

boonsho bran

boorr flour

boorr gainq cleft palate

bokti mold

bor ashy, cry

bolol mold; rotten

bololiy past tense of bolol

borowo to try, example, sample

borowoy try

bori to make (someone) cry

borboro powder

borboro'o the powders

borjeb wallet

borso suitcase, bag

boss cripple

bosto mailbox

bostole delivery; mail carrier

bostoley postwoman; mailwoman

bostolow mailman; postman

boubsi fast; quickly

bouri to make (someone or something) ashy

bobouqle an arrogant word for "throat"

booh to fill

boohi to fill (something) up

boohe full, filled up

boohsomiy full, filled up

boosto blankets

boug finish

bougiy finished

bougtiy *feminine* finished

boulow noise, yell

bouor pumpkin

boud boundary, protective fence

bowb devour or to hug food for oneself

bowiy past of *bowb*

bowzhd jump

bowzhiy jumped

bowzhdti skip

bowzhdtiyairi goalkeeper

brig second

brig'o the seconds

brra dancing zone; dancing area

bubu dumb, can't speak

bubun gastropod

bubunqkajirrow snail

budd baseball bat, hitting bat

bulbuli to ruin

bunni *lexicon* "brown"

burdtam party

burdtamiy partied

burburi destroy

bunn coffee bean

bur stone

burji great luck or fortune

burrkaiti adobe

buru cornstarch; cornmeal

burus hammer

burs to chase

burso chase

bus bus

bus jrhoji bus stop

bushi disease

buskud biscuit

busto dusts

buthale an unfortunate person

buuqa *lexicon* "noise"

buwb fly

buwa to say fly in plural

buwi to make (something) fly

buwiy flied

buwko is when a tire has a hole

bwa expression; "is" or "are"

byllbyll spicy; chili

byrr to ride on, away to access

byrrbyrr to ride on

C

caawi *lexicon* help

cabb *lexicon* drink

caruur *lexicon* "children"

China China (pronounced slightly different)

Chines Chinese

choqolato chocolate

chorai draw

chorayiy drew

chorayoye drawing

ceyli *lexicon* defend

D

daar to infect, to carry out from

daad river

daal to crave for food

daaley a person that is greedy with food

dabal stupid, dumb

dacuoos peacock

dacuxa curtain

daf grab

daff tambourine, small drum

dafufi spin

dafufia *plural* to say spin

dagarsongh fasting charity

dafufio dragonfly

dagiga minute

dahab gold

dahabmaley goldfish

dahab qozhe gold digger

dai an expression of anger; "Quickly!"

daiad dwarf

daibb fire, power

daidd *singular* human, people

daidd'o the people

daidd aanq cannibal

daiddba no one; no people

daiddfeer greedy person

daiddkasto everybody

daiji to put (something) off, calm down

daimi turn off

daimiy past of daimi

dain to say or tell directly to (something) to turn itself off

daigg get off, land, live

daiggan environment

daiggdaigg immediately

daiggmad district

daigal war

daigale warrior

dairess neighbor

dair winter to spring

dairbi wall

daizho plural of *daidd*

daizhow you people

daiy look, watch

daiy bauh to look, check, just see

daithal to work on (something) constantly until it is done, strenuous

dair fall, winter season

daji to watch over cattle while they eating or to take cattle to eat; graze

dal country; geography

dalbo select, order, decide

daldal to pick multiple (things) on floor or ground

daldal to hog in

daldalin to whine or complain on and on

dallaya umbrella

daleeg massage

dalhees tourist

daliji devour or to ground

dalol cavity

dambe after, next, last

dambeay to make (something) to be at last

dambeel basket

dambeelbloun basketball

dambouy behave

dameen not smart, dumb

damer donkey

damerfarrow zebra

damooji to close or squeeze tightly

dammunq speed

dammumi to speed up

damurk asphalt

dandarus a housewife that trains a new housewife how to be a good housewife

dango popcorn

danggal clef palate

dangga hair scarf; hair veil; Somali hair scarf

dan accident

damiy past tense of *dan*

danmey portray

dann business, something to do

danneso to look or decide what to do

dannesozhiy past tense of *danneso*

danyer baboon

danyerow a name that is compared to a baboon

dar turn on, to set on

darba noun of darbai

darbai to hit back harder

dardaar message

dariiq avenue

daran meaningful, to be worse

daraw underestimate

darawiy underestimated

darre not, without, un, less

darrer walk

darrere to be going

darreriy past tense of *darer*

darreroye walking

darrerne going (used with "we")

darreroyne walking (used with "we")

darrerso walk away

darrertena going (used with "you guys")

darreroyena walking (used with "you guys")

darrerte *feminine* going

darem feel, nerve

daremiy felt

daremtiy *feminine* felt

darenq *noun* feeling

darewal driver

darisha window

darranq strange, danger

darrey impractical, useless

darr to add more, to couple up

darrsizhiy gotten worse

darul drill

daryel care, to take care

daryelqazhe caretaker

dashh diner, dining room or place

dauad loyal, honest, good person

dauas flip-flops

dauawo trial, to sue

dauawoy sue

daumau interest, immerse, intrigue

daumag to be suddenly doubted

daurr matter or wrong

dawa *plural* rig

dawal swim

dawal swimming pool, swimming

dawb rig, to set a trap

dawiy rigged

dauwa chemical

dawwel heavy wind, bad spirit

Daood or **Daud** male name; sweetheart; (American) David

dawol lid, to cover or close

dauworumo toothpaste

dawou medicine; medication

daweuad personality, attitude

dawouy remedy; cure

dawoy to slave, drudge, to burden

dawwo lexicon "behind" or "ass"

dayh neglect or leave

dayy late

dayyman lateness; tardiness

dek dock

dek'o the docks

dizhd refuse

dizhiy refused

deef booger; phlegm

deeg roster

deeg'o the rosters

deeg doro roster

deen religion

deeneya riddle

deerito straight

deyha size

deag to fit

deagiy fitted

dembi sin

dembile sinner

deues to burp

deueso burp

deymi to lend or loan

deyn debt, loan

deyn tzee the debt (used in situation)

deyr reach

deyriy reached

dha middle, center

dha tzee the middle

dhaar oath

dhaaro to swear, to commit

dhab to strongly hold or stick to (someone or something)

dhacga *lexicon* "rock or stone"

dhad episode

dhad yal episodes

dhadhan mindless

dhadhanji imitate

dhaf to leave (someone or something) alone

dhafin olive

dhafiy left alone

dhafar to stay up all night

dhafoor the front of a cheek

dhag wash

dhagag move

dhagagiy moved

dhaggala anchovy

dhagiy washed

dhahal inheritance

dhahan freeze, cold

dhahir *noun* to be ablated, ablutionary

dhaeef weak

dhagal culture

dhaig hear

dhaigiy heard

dhaigal bride's maid, best man

dhaigenso listen

dhaigwole deaf

dhail dance, play

dhaiji snake

dhaireg to be full, not hungry

dhairegiy full

dhagan tradition

dhakso quick

dhal born, kid

dhalyow children

dhalad native

dhaley childish

dhaleydhaley childishness

dhal'o the kids

dhalali to melt (something)

dhalaliy melted

dhalasho relative

dhallo glass, glass bottle

dhalli score

dhallyiy scored

dhalashan birth certificate

dhalasha birth, birth date

dhalynyar youth

dhaman entire

dhamai complete

dhamayiy completed

dhamaytiy completed (referring to a female)

dhamaystur to finish what is left of (something), to finish the rest of (something)

dhamazhd ultimate, end

dhamazhd kee the ultimate

dhamazhiy ended, done, over

dhambal chop

dhamiy drank

dhan whole

dhanaw sour

dhanq or **dham** drink

dhaunn way

dhaqa-dhaqa hide-and-seek

dhap serious, for real

dharr cloth

dharar to be in a hurry or in haste

dharar hunggur fast food

dhararoye hurrying, in a hurry, the act of urgency

dharawo worm, earthworm

dharbanyo slap

dharer drool, dorky, weenie

dharerle a person that drools

dharr'o the clothes

dharub stain of booger or dirt

dharanq piece of cloth

dhau to con

dhauiy past of *dhau*

dhauan liquid

dhauiy past tense of *dhau*

dhawag a tree liquid that's dried

dhawah injury

dhawahiy past tense of *dhawah*

dhedhail play

dhedhail playground

dhedhail dhul playground

dhedhyymi taste

dhedin bait

dheug VCR, DVD player, player

dheeb to peep, peek

dheebo peep

dheebbogg or **boggdheeb** peephole

dheaf peacefulness, development

dheamo to go or get (somewhere) early

dheeg blood

dheeg'o the bloods

dheegkarr blood pressure, high blood pressure,

dheg to stick with (something or someone)

dhegdheg sticky

dheh say, be, do

dhehiy past tense of *dheh*

dheji to stick (something) on (something)

dhenyyg tasty, sense of taste

dhear long; far

dhearai to make (something) long

dher tall, height

dheyji sickness or nausea of hunger eyes

dheyjis *noun* sickness or nausea of hunger eyes

dhi to fall, fail, expire, happen

dhi fall season

dhyiy fell

dhib problem, bother

dhifir belt

dhig to put or write down

dhigow author

dhihir slug

dhilmanyo wasp; mosquito

dhiib pass, handover, pay, or give

dhiiqad *lexicon* "mud"

dhiiwiy past tense of *dhiib*

dhiir bamboo

dhilgo bed bug

dhilo slut

dhig to write, to put down, to act

dhigow writer

dhiiqar or **malandaryel** daycare

dhinmi to hurt for more where it's hurting

dhinq or **dhim** reduce

dhimiy reduced

dhinqtiy *feminine* reduced

dhini side

dhini'o the sides

dhini darrer sidewalk

dhim or **dhin** to die

dhimbi sink, to put undr water

dhimbil ember

dhimbildaibb ember

dhimishosarir death bed

dhimisho death; dying

dhimizhiy dead

dhimizhow something or someone that dies easily

dhimo die

dhimozha die (used when there is more than one)

dhinan daughter, girl

dhinan tzo some girl

dhinanyey *feminine* you girl, kiddo

dhirid sweat

dhirif anger

dhirifiy got angry, angered

dhiriftiy *feminine* got angry, angered

dhirifinte *feminine* angry

dhirifinye angry (used with "I am," "he," "we")

dhirifinyena angry (used with "they")

dhis build

dhismo building

dhisow builder

dhiwato trouble

dhiwey bugger

dhofor forehead

dhoqod stupid

dhonggo kiss (used with "you")

dhonq when a battery is dead or powerless, dead battery

dhoog absorb, suck, smoke

dhooge a person who smokes, smoke, smoker

dhoogow smoker

dhoogiy past tense of *dhoog*

dhoogtiy *feminine* past tense of *dhoog*

dhour to leave (someone/something) alone

dhour to save something at last

dhow hit, near

dhowagg floor, level

dhran naked; nude

dhub mute

dhubsi to mute

dhufo *lexicon* "hit"

dhuffais position, hiding position

dhufoori a big fool

dhugg memory, to heed

dhuggso heed

dhuggsozha *plural* heed

dhuggunso listen

dhuggunsizha *plural* listen

dhuhoo liquid or fluid that comes out from tube of bond

dhuhul charcoal

dhuji knot

dhujyiy knotted

dhukay earwax

dhule brown

dhul ground

dhumiy got lost

dhumo hide, escape

dhumozha hide, escape (used with "you guys")

dhunq to get lost

dhunqtiy *feminine* got lost

dhunji swallow

dhukksi the act of eating everything or to make everything not exist anymore

dhukksia to say "eat everything" to more than one person

dhur save, to keep (something)

dhurow a person who saves (money or something)

dhus fart

dhuub thin

dhudhuub narrow

dhuun throat

dhuuni a person who is selfish with food

dhuur ant

dhuur'o the ants

dhuri ache, sore, hurt

dhusug dirty, dirt

dhusug'o the dirties

dhusun ass

dhusun goud asshole

dhusunmol deep ass, asshole

dhyggdhyggo earring

dhygg ear

dhygg'o the ears

dhyggoule deaf

dhyyg to bite

dhyygiy past tense of *dhyyg*

dhyyn to taste

dhyynsi to make (someone or something) taste

dibbid when a place is quite and have no existing lives

diffau defend, defender

dig lecture, to inform

digir peas

digir agaar green peas

digtoun attention

digri some Somali culture that singed in Islam

diiney chafer beetle

diir warm

dil kill

dile killer

dillig vomit

dindarrey wasteful, pointless

dir send, submit

dir to give a call

diwi bull

diwi'o the bulls

diyar ready

diyari to make (something) ready

diidin turtle

diin the level of the Quran

diyrr to turn (two people or some things) against each other

don quest, request

donqfalio swings

donq back: the rear part of body

donq hill

donqfaar pig

donqlaf backbone

doob fry, bake

dool dive

doomi to tear (something) down, demolish

doomiy past tense of *doomi*

doog bury

doos to dent, to knock down

doosiy past tense of *doos*

dogonq idiot

dogonyow called by idiot person

dogonyey feminine of *dogonyow*

dol cake

doraduured peafowl

doro chicken

dorogwisa a person who do drugs

dorogwo drug

dorr choice

dorrosho election, selection

dorro select, elect

dou conversation, admonition

doua bless (*dua*)

douad fox

douai *verb* bless

dowh nonsense; rubbish

doun boat

dounq or **doum** drowsy

douni canoe

dowlad government

dowladle governor

dozhd to speak up, take action, or fight

dozhiy past tense of *dozhd*

dtuko pray

dubb tail

dubbadhde raccoon

dubbgodd scorpion

dudd to scoot over

dudooma termite hill or mound

dugg bend over, an old person

duggiy bent

duggoshinq senior adult

duwgag inhuman; beast, creature

duhur *noun* midday, noon prayer

duhurcui to be obvious or having connection toward the prayer of noon

duggowiy got old

dukanq convenience store, shop

dukan'o the stores

duxsi Islamic religious school

dul *noun* crowd, tribe

dulsho public

dumar gal

dumashi brother-in-law or sister-in-law (only the opposite sex can call the other "dumashi")

duna map

duul crowd

doon thread

doon'o the threads

dur to stab with a dagger

durug move over

duub record, wrap, roll

doof wrestle

duur forest, jungle

durduur a forest or a place that looks like forest

dyaura plane; airplane

dyaura jill jet lag

dyaradaiggain airport

dyggdygg to bother or pick on (someone)

E

e or **'a** do, are, is (used in the end of adjectives and verbs)

eab shame, disgrace, discreet

eaid very

eal water well

eeh her, she

eeh abasheh herself

eelaley sheep

eemanq the appreciation of having something without wanting for more

eeyo they, them

eeyo abasho themselves

eeyo kulli or **eeyo kullisho** all of them

eeyogu *lexicon* "they" or "them"

eeyow hurry, soon

eeyoweeyow hurry

eeyowtey hurry up

eranq raw, unripe

ei me

eiaa variant of "wow"

eiadu *lexicon* "she/her"

eid holiday, celebration

eizho to celebrate

eizho celebrations, holidays

eid mubarak happy holiday

eid muwaraka holiday gift; holiday giveaway

elleunq rehearsal

elbor airport

elacuelo deers

engouni *adjective* different

enjaig to dry

enjaigiy dried

eray *lexicon* word

ento same, alike

eoyd voice

eryamo fog

euy? did?

euyna? did? (used with "they" and "you guys")

ewaid ever

ewair empty, zero

ewyylou somebody

ey dog

ey kee the dog

eyduured wild dog; jackal

ey'o the dogs

ey yal kee the dogs

ezhd blame

F

faali to say good thing about (something or someone), to support

faar a disgusting substance that grows on a dirt

fack to open wide

facksi open wide

fachaq wet

faddryyshain rice and beans cooked together

fadhi huddle, seat

fadheuaw keep sitting

fadhew or **fadhewso** sit

fadhewsizhiy sat

fadhewsitiy *feminine* sat

fadlan please

fag to dig or look throough

fageer poor

fahan or **faham** understand

fahamiy understood

fahamtiy *feminine* understood

faid open

faino glad, gloat

faizhow opener

fal to hoe a (garden), do

falebo ivy

faliy past tense of *fal*

falo the act of going to hoe a (garden), to do

famil family

fana gap

fanan artist

fann fang

fantin to gloat

farah happy

farahiy got happy

farcuad celebration

farangfar woodchuck

farangfaria gopher

farantijairi refrigerator

farawo space, room

fareeg scratch, to take apart

fareegiy past tense of *fareeg*

farinq brake

farli kindly

farjhi splash, to splash away

farmo cheese

farr finger

farryarey pinkie finger; pinkie

farranti ring

farrdiir lukewarm, tepid

farrkaiti fork

farr'o the fingers

farsho art

farshohowll artwork

farur lip

fas beautiful, perfect, nice

faslinte beautiful

faslinye *masculine* beautiful

fassal grade

faslin petroleum jelly; vaseline

fassa permission, excuse

fash to be embarrassed

fasho wound dressing

fathoye want

fathur or **fathuthi** a person who is disrespectful and troublesome to others

fathuthi to treat or do disrespect stuff to (something or someone)

Fatima female name; wean

fathiil rake

fattash to dig or look through into (things) to find (something)

Fartun female name; lucky

Fatuma variant of *Fatima*

fatura small car

fatura tartanq race car

fauizho advantage, use, value

faye fine

fayfai sprinkle, light rain

fayhle nice

fayhley female name; nice or beautiful

fayte *feminine* fine

fazhdiy had, could have, could have had, want

fazhd to want

fazhiy wanted

fazhiy masculine of *fazhdiy*

feeg peel

feegiy peeled

feer greed

feeri to view, inspect, or check out

fel line

fero iron

festo fiesta, carnival, party

feynus kerosene lamp, lantern

feyl compete

feyloye competing

fiaw to cure, to be healthy

fiawye cured, healthy

fiawanq health

fiawouy cure

fiawte *feminine* cured, fine

fian best, greatest

fiid bud

fiijhi the act of getting things or people out of a place

fiin bead

fiiqso sniff

fiiqsizhiy sniffed

fiish eye boogers, eye discharge

fin fin

filan an act of comparison between two or more people that are same age or size

film film

film'o the films, films

fikir think

fikiriy thought

firiq sip

firiqsiy to sip, sip

firiqsiyiy sipped

firiqsiytiy *feminine* sipped

filfil hot pepper

filfil mazhow black pepper

filar bow, the weapon bow

finq pimple

finqfinq acne; rash

firr kind of people; race

firimbi whistle

fissir translate

fiuil when someone doesn't want to do something because of another person not doing it or want to do what the other person is doing

fioro flower

fizno the act of somebody breaking two people's relationship apart or bringing civil war into peace environment

foal labour; childbirth

foufi to take or spread

foki release

fokid fugitive

fokizhiy got away

fol *lexicon* "face"

folio tortilla

foondi mechanic

fuundi act of fixing bad magic

fouri to whistle

fowzh float

fowzhoye floating

fowzhoyte *feminine* floating

fowzhiy past tense of *fowzh*

foor fat, fat body

foosto barrel

forjo tease

forno oven

forow plastic drinking cup

frag a lap made by folding one's cloth like basket

frais horse

frais'o the horses

fudd poof

ful to be on a (ride or something)

ful a ride

fulgaiddi to flip, to turn over

fulan passenger

fuley coward, craven, scaredy-cat

fulthes easy

fulthudd flexible, simple

fulthuzhai to be flexible or fast

furrung to tell (something) to open itself up

furruma to tell (some things) to open themselves up

funano shirt

furrso escape, getaway

furrsizhiy past tense of *furrso*

furrsitiy *feminine* past tense of *furrso*

furrsa chance, opportunity

furr unlock, divorce

furr a head cover of (bottle, jar, can)

furr open

fura key

fura'o the keys

fura yal keys

furangfuria beaver

furfuria couscous

furun or **mauawis** an open two side cloak worn by Somali or muslim man that covers from the waist to below

futo ass

fuud soup

fuurafuura beans soup

fydd dowry

fyrr rib

G

Gaal Christian

Gaala *feminine* Christian

Gaal mazhow black Christian

Gaal adhdan white Christian

gaajo famish, hunger

garob a divorced woman

gab short

gabisaar scarf

gad to wait on, espy

gaddonq flip

gaddomi to flip (something)

gaddomiy flipped

gahabo tramp, woman who had sex with many different men

gahar suffer, burden

gahar difficult situation

gahawa coffee, ground coffee

gahs horn

gaigi today

gaibdho young lady, girl

gaibo to duck

gaibsi to slam

gaid tree

gaid jabati roller mill; dough roller

gaiddi to turn, roll, switch, flip

gaif to miss, fail to hit, dodge

gaigso or **adkeso** endure, to take pain

gaig noun of *gaigso*

gaili to put in, to absorb

gaimbi to ditch (someone or something)

gaimbairr throne/chair

gainq throw, shoot, dump, pitch

gaintal missile

gaimow thrower, pitcher

gairad the day before yesterday

gairr chin, beard

gairgar state of helping out

gairi giraffe

gais angle

gaiss hornlike, horn

gaissi yak

gaiwyrr girl

gaiwyrrsahib girlfriend

gaiwyrreygawyrrey barbie doll

gaiwyrreymanya mermaid

gal enter, go in, into

galman entrance

galab afternoon

galamudo Somali dish that made out of flour and boiled up with soup

galas class

gallus button

Gamar variant of *Qamar*, moon

gambalel bell

gamun arrow

gamun'o arrows

gandolo a male sheep

ganjo knob, handle

ganjela gate

ganjelahaayow gatekeeper

gannah suspend

gannahiy suspended, charged

gar *noun* right, point, justice

garab arm

garab'o the arms

garaj garage

garangar roll, roller

gargar the act of taking side for battle

garbosaar men scarf

garbo shoulder

garbo'o the shoulders

gareer eagle

gari truck, vehicle

garigauan wheelbarrow

garonq field

garran muscle shirt

garrey to handle or make (something) to happen

garriir vibrate, quake

garriiroye vibrating

garsorre *lexicon* "judge"

gas gas

gasac *noun* "can"

gasac faid can opener

gasac faid kee the can opener

gash to wear

gashan shield

gasho wear

gashizha *plural* wear

gashqol wareroom

gathd sell, to buy

gath aih will sell

gathiy sold

gatho to buy

gathizha *plural* buy

gathizhiy *masculine* bought

gathitiy bought

gazh aih will be espying

gathal *lexicon* "behind"

gaual dear

gauan hand

gauan guley left hand

gauan mithig right hand

gaurrgaurra *noun* the act of looking for trouble, fuss

gaurrgaurra guilt

gawal fragment, part, piece

gazhud red

geyl camel

geyl'o the camels

geylowgulalow old term for "camel"

geyl yal camels

geysi brave

gilan a girl who became a woman

girgir *noun* mixed colors

giss "Screw you."

gishan young unmarried woman

gjey deliver, take to

go at some time, at time, when a time (used with singular pronoun)

go rather

godd to bend

gohrri behead

gohrriyiy beheaded

gohrriow beheader

gorgoro a long underskirt; underskirt

gozhiy past tense of *godd*

gof junk

gongfo casual cloth

gongfoso to wear casual clothes or to make cloth into casual cloth

gonji limp

gono skirt

guzhd pay back, avenge

golof trashy; broken

goo winter

goodi *noun* general, commissioned officer

googoob thunder

gool or **gugool** to make something/someone scare

goonda *feminine* pigeon

goondo pigeon

goorr keep saying

goor evaporate

goorma *lexicon* when

gooriy evaporated

goos penis

gorgortin negotiate, bargain

gouy jaw

gonq the pointy part of the back of a head

gorwan negotiate

goryanq tapeworm

goud hole

gouhan decision

gouni apart from, apart

gour time

gouo sheet

gouo yal sheets

goumar sneak talk, gossip like

gow edge

gowanq trap place, trap area

gowan'o plural of *gowanq*

gowd piece of cloth

gowol state, state of a country

goy cut, rip off

gogoy to cut piece by piece

golshi sofa

grram crunch

gud circumcise

gudbi act of passing through, transfer

gudomie mayor

guffur waste of liquid

guguwb burned, burned food

gulgulumoye mumbling

gumais owl

gumo a small forest dove

guma dubb dhear a small forest dove that has long tail

gunn bundle

guntino kit

gurban bongo drum

gurey left position

guri apartment

gurr act of cutting off weed or plant from the ground, weeding

gushi pride

guud when a head have tail; tail of a head

guul success

guur to settle, to move to a place and make it home, marriage

guuriy past tense of *guur*

guurowmaudaiggow nomad

gutha inside; in

guthae insider

guthakouy income

guthanq crawl

guthiy *masculine* past tense of *gud*

guthub cross over

guwb burn

guwiy burned

guwus a flat and thick homemade Somali bread

gyrrfi clove

gyyley corn kernel, kernel

gyylgyyla arid, dry and hot place, desert

H

haa yes

haar shit

haasid unkind person; evil mind person

haay to keep, hold, have

haaxay or **haa daiy** expression; "yes, that's right"

hab style

habad one, each, into part, each one

Habiba female name; beloved

habazhd bullet

habazhd'o bullets, the bullets

hadaa an expression; "already"

hannani to take care of

hadhow later

hadhow "then" or "so what"

hadaytey early

hadayey earlier

haddi now

haddina again

hadee if

hadiad present; gift

hafad village

hafadhew *lexicon* "come sit"

hafis office

haflad get-together, event

hagaji to organize and clean

hagajyiy organized

hagajitiy *feminine* organized

hagg right, acceptable

hagg gais right angle

haggdawo bad person

haghay drizzle

haib shore

haid behind

haih an expression; "so" or "then"

hais song

haiwaidd chest

haizhahaizho backwards

halaag jeopardy; jeopardize

hafad town; district

hahl to be found

hahliy past tense of *hahl*

hajheen caterpillar

Haji male name; skillful

Hajia female name; skillful

hajiin dough

hal one, uni, single

halad situation

halal ritually pure

halbaig mile

hal bogol one hundred

hal gour one time

hallin self of (seed)

halis risky, dangerous

hal jair one time

hallawo some things, some

hal marr one time

hal dhini one side

halkaas *lexicon* "there"

halkaun *Lexicon* "here"

hamal labour, work

hamali labourer

hamaqso yawn

hamaqsizhiy yawned

hambal leaf

hambogo spinach

hammad gossip

hambali congrats; to congratulation

hambalio congratulation

hamila pregnant

hamweenq lail midnight

hamweenq night

hamweenq gumais night owl

hamweenq kaun this night, tonight

hamweenq kaas that night

hamweenq mugdi dark night

hamweenqsamel midnight

hanag very angry, mad, furious

hanagiy past tense of *hanag*

hangfar wind

han tank

hanjo gum

hankaar curse

hanqararia millipede

hanqqarif to scratch deep

hanshab a handful of (things)

hanshab quo some, a handful of (things)

hanshab tzo *feminine* some, a handful of (things)

hanshabdhow applaud, clap

hansho junk paper

hanoonq pain

hanooniy been in pain

hanoonqtiy *feminine* been in pain

hannung so much, so

hannung hardly

hanqas ink

hapsi jail

haraf letter: the alphabet letter

haraf'o the letters

harafad sentence

haranq impure (*haram*)

hargag nappy, to be tight, curly tight

harkawim stuck

harkawimiy got stuck

hareef dude

hareef quo a/some dud

hariif juke, dribble

harran yard, a ground that is surrounding a house or building

haranti kick

harby to try hard, to fight with

hariig to make a line or circle on the ground

hariigiy past tense of *hariig*

hariigin a hand-drawn line, circle, etc. on the ground

harra a round protected place or section, an area by surrounded by fence

harreay to put (something) in or away

harti husband

hathag rope

hathag'o the ropes

hathag bobowzhd or **bowzhd hathag** jump rope

Hassan male name; proper

hasha wow, bravo

hashish marijuana, weed, cannabis

hassu to remember, to remind

hassuso try to remember, recall, flash back

hassusinte remember, recall

hassusinye *masculine* remember, recall

hatta even, too

hatheeg a clean person, neat person

hau let

haug sweep

hauginq broom

hauxs to be thin

hauxsiy past tense of *hauxs*

hawaar beshrew, curse

hawath weather

Hawa female name; desire; (American) Eve

hawaji curry powder

hawaji byllbyll chilli powder

hawaji dhudhuub cumin

hawal grave

hawal'o graves, graveyard, cemetery, tomb

hawank act of by force

hawanka an expression; "forcefully"

hawarr *lexicon* "mother"

hawb hug

haweay organize

hawi to pick (things) on floor or ground

hawis dustpan

hawiy hugged

hawoug to cover

hawougiy past tense of *hawoug*

hawug corn

hawug'o the corns

hayaiy is a signal for "watch out" or "run"

haye hi, hello

haye *interjection* wow

hayye okay, yeah

hazhal talk

hazhaloye talking

hazhaliy talked

hazhd steal

hazhdiy *feminine* stole

hazha *plural* steal

hazhiy stole

hel cinnamon

heer shave

hees to get tired of (someone or something) or to miss (someone or something) so badly, depends on the preposition

heesiy past tense of *hees*

hehr home

herbadia people who live in forest

hergaib mucus, flu

hes sing

hesow or **hesoy** singer

hesey or **hestoy** female singer

hesoye *masculine* singing

hesoyte singing

heyrgyrr stay over, morning

heyrgyrrthyy "Good morning" and the reply "heyrgyrrthyy"

heyrgyrrthyyna "good morning" (used when there is more than one person)

heyshi to settle, to agree

heyshis agreement, treaty

heyr not to come or go with, to stay apart

hige next

hiir wave

hillai to hurt, to mess, or to maim (something) up

hilib meat

hiliwole butcher

hillimo dream

hillio nightmare

hilmanq forget

hilmamiy forgot

hilmanqtiy *feminine* forgot

hilow miss, regret resulting from loss

hilowiy past tense of *hilow*

hindig star

hindigmaley starfish

hingathi to spell out

hingathioye spelling

hingathyiy past tense of *hingathi*

hingo hiccup

hinjhis sneeze

hinjhisoye or **hinjhisozhoye** sneezing

hir to tie, to shut

hirhir strangle

hirtenq *noun* tie

hisawb count, accounting

hisawbtin to think about, to think

hisawiy past tense of *hasawb*

hismad courtesy, respect

hirab morning

hithid root, vein

hiuhrr manly stomach, manly belly

hixqi maggot

hixqi'o the maggots

hoa "here, take it"

hooyo *lexicon* "mother"

hoazha "here, take it" (referring to more than one person)

hocg to scratch in joyful way

hodi phrase "Is anyone there/ home?"

hocgiy past tense of *hogg*

hol scrape

holiy scraped

hoingh an expression of disgust or disgrace

honk honk

hombar dolphin

hoob weapon

hoogami to program or control

hoong for the sake of, just for

hoorr or **wuirr** never or to dare not to

hoos the act of throwing a food party and blessing for a dead person

hor first, front

horey a front person, a person who is next

hore earlier, ancient time

hordhowo to bump into (something or someone)

hordhowozhiy bumped

horan in the past, earlier time

horhaay lead

horhaayoye leading

horhaayle leader

horyaal title, topic

hos down, under

hosrhorr download

hotel hotel

hosh shade, shadow

hosgash underwear

houg force, muscle

houl club, usually a club for wedding

houxla animal

houwi ocean

houw yes (used to reply when a person's name is being called)

houlof loosen

howan cloud

howay lullaby

howll task, employment, job, work

howllbele workless, not responsible

howllhaay employer

howlle employee

howllawe unemployed

hoy hey

hubno element

hubso to make sure

hubte sure

huff scrub

huffiy scrubbed

hulli yet

humbo foam

hunjhuf saliva

hunn ugly

hunn bad, unpleasant

hundur sleep

hunduroye *masculine* asleep, sleeping

hunduroyte asleep, sleep

hundurmo *noun* sleep

hunggur food

hungguri meal

hunggur aanq eat food

hunsul elbow

hukkun to control; to rule

hukkumad regulation

hurdo (*lexicon*) *noun* "sleep"

hurday a person who sleeps a lot

hur flame

hursi set on fire

hursinye to be very hungry for anything, on fire

hursinte feminine of *hursinye*

huriy past tense of *hur*

hurbi to paddle, paddle

hurbunq paddle for food

huroodd ground turmeric or yellowish subtance that is put on the face, thanaka, facial mask

huroye flaming, to be on fire

Hussein or **Hussain** male name; handsome

huur sweat

huwb to close or seal

hyyl *verb* grant

I

i don't

idd *lexicon* "home" or "family"

iggar lad

ijar rent

ijo nail, like thumbnail or toenail

ijo jhar nail clipper

il eyeball

ilo eyeballs

ilali watch over

ilalyiy *masculine* past tense of *ilali*

ilalitiy past tense of *ilali*

ilao *intransitive preposition* with

ilao to (used with "talk," "speak")

ilaojir ilaojir to be with

ilaojire with

Illahey God (Allah)

Illaheyow God (used to talk directly to God)

illa except, but

ilbab door

ilbah a person who thinks he/she is smart and likes to take advantage of others

illin tear

illan henna

iliq tooth

iliq'o the teeth

ilm child

ilmi knowledge, education

ilm'o the children

ilmow you children

illow *lexicon* forget

imaan belief, faith

Imam a Muslim who leads prayer

iman *lexicon* "come"

Imzigula singular of *Wazigula*

inanq son, boy

inanq quo some boy

inanyow you boy, kiddo

indho eye

indho'o the eyes

indhole blind

indhoduub blindfold

indholedhini blindside

Ingiriis English

in acquaint, to where, to

ing for

injaiso excuse, pardon

in weyr to call or to call (someone or something) out loud

injir louse

innay aunt

inni holy spirit

inqir deny

insha Allah (*Arabic*) "God willing," "If Allah wills it."

intaas there

intahan test

intahan wein big test, exam

inteyh which place, where

intee before, instead, while

inti here

inti ka bah leave from here or go from here

inyaw no (used by children)

irbid needle

ir sky

irri sun

irrirewb sunblock

irrid exit, entry

ir kee the sky

is together, each other, be

is self, selves

isbattorre *lexicon* "inspector"

is gaiddi to roll or flip

isgow nice smell, scent

Isa a name of Jesus

isbunq sponge

isbunyo sponges

isfeyl competition

isha two or three hours before midnight, before midnight prayer

ishacui to be obvious or having connection toward the prayer of before midnight

isjir be cautious

isjoug suit

iskajoug pair of cloth that have the same colour and design

is ka darr sum up or pair up (some things or people)

is ka dhaf leave or forget (someone or something)

iskalawb to mix (things) together

iskajir beware

iskarbo boot

iskerso *noun* bluff

iskouris rascal

islanq a Muslim man

islan Muslim women

Isha female name; night prayer

ising you guys, y'all

is raha "Go together."

istaag stop, stand

Istafirullah (Arabic) "Forgive me, God (Allah)."

Ithinku or **isinku** *lexicon* "you guys"

istairinq steering wheel

is tuma fight each other

issawi conjurer, necromancer

iyah huh, what

iyal a young person who likes to have fun or goof around; child

iyar kid, play

iyaroye kidding

iyartoy *lexicon* player

iyo and

J

jaasi act of avenging, become disobedience or to pay back somehow

jabati a round flat Somali bread that is usually made of flour and cooked in a pan

jabouy embrace, hug

jahwarer trauma

jahanama hellfire or hell

jairaijai admire, fond of

jaiwey contagion

jaka coat, jacket

jallato popsicle

jama holy

jama biyo holy water

jamauad university, college

jannah heaven, paradise

jannaso to bless or praise a dead body so the dead body's spirit can go to heaven

Jarair weyne Somalis, Somali Bantu and Shambar'o

jalal desert

jaranjar stairs

jaranjara ladder

jarr checkers, chess

jathiizhd fresh

jaseera island

jahil a very ignorant person

jat khat

jawwi habitat

jai a road or a street that has gravel but has no tar

jeb pocket

jeeran neighbour

jeerr *lexicon* "thigh"

jeezhd to drag, to pull

jeezho to say drag (something) for or by yourself

jeezho go away; scram

jeezhizha to say drag (something) for or by yourselves

jeewi to say okay to whatever

jeag small bucket

jeg check, bank check

jega fade haircut

jeg'o the checks

jaimis jeans

jer hippopotamus

jes chalk

jesta header, hitting ball with head

jeuel love

jeyzhd to refer or imply, to be awake, to go or head to (somewhere)

jhab piece

jhab'o the pieces

jhabtiy *feminine* broke, broken

jhar cut, shear

jhaiwi to break

jhaiwiy it's broke

jher feel ashamed, disappoint

jheri to make someone/something disapointed

jhijhib chick, chicken

jhijhib doro little chicken

jhifo lie down

jhiwisa anaconda

jibar exponent

jicg bleach

jicg'o the bleaches

jid street, path

jid monq big street

jiffi lard

jig to hold or hold back

jihad a holy war fought by Muslims to defend themselves and their religion

jiil generation

jiir mouse

jiir'o mice

jilal summer

jillauh the first immigrants to Somalia, they mostly have soft hair

jikko kitchen

jilbo *noun* lap

jilalbib a loose-fitting cloth that covers the entire body of a woman, except the face and the hands

jilib knee

jilibjhaibso or **jilibo** kneel

jimbar bunk

jimbar sarir bunk bed

jimmil boulder

jinq size, fit, even

jinni phantasm, evil spirit, evil genie

jinni ghost

jinni hankaret a unknown evil spiritual creature

jinnijinni cartoon

jinnole crazy

jijin bracelet

jijin'o the bracelets

jimil a giane rock

jir hip

jir heft, body, bulk

jiranjir earthquake

jirinte sick

jirinye *masculine* sick

jiro sickness, sick

jirif *lexicon* "pinch"

jirow sicko, psycho

jirr old, at, in, to be going on

jierre exist

jiur to turn

jiuraw turn

jiura *noun* turn

jiurai to make (something) turn

jiuss bruise

jirzhe true of something, reality, exist

joosto nothing is missing, exact

joujira mattress

journal journal

jrhog height

jrhog to stand, stay, stop

jrhog at (used with "you," "she," "you guys," "we")

jrhogaw stay

jrhoge to be (somewhere); present

jrhogiy stood, stayed

jrhogso stand up, stop

jrhogsizhiy stood up

jrhogsitiy *feminine* stood up

jrhoji to make (something) stop

jugg injury, bump

jumai straighten, to make (something) fit or even

jumayiy straightened

jumaysinye *masculine* straightened

jumaysinte *feminine* straightened

jumaytiy *feminine* straightened

Jummah Friday

juunia burlap sack

juwab answer

K

ka from, on, off, about, than, around, away, to

ka on, on top of (something)

ka from (used to imply "from him," "from her," "from you guys")

ka than (used to imply "rather than her," "rather than them," "rather than him")

kaalay *lexicon* come

kaas that

kaathi pee

kaathigalenq bladder

ka bah leave from

ka bah inti leave from here

kabriid *lexicon* match

ka daar to dip

ka daaro dip

ka daaria *plural* dip

ka darr to add, to couple up

ka dhaf to leave (something or someone) where it is at

kadib after

ka hige to be next to

ka higte *feminine* to be next to

kahor before

ka kyh move away

ka jir include, to be in

kabil coincide, agree

kaftan or **kaftam** joke

kaftamoye joking

kaftamow joker

kai to hide, hiding place

kailaibb a person that has no manners

kaimaithi oat

kaiwaish cabbage

kai yal *noun* plural of *kai*

kau *masculine* your (used with things)

kairkair shiver

ka yaran at least

kyrrkyrri wild boar

kakanq hard

kakananq hardest, so hard

kakanai to make (something) hard

kakka some hard Somalian food that is made out of flour and fried in oil

kalbi mind

kalle other

kalled another, else

kalmos *noun* help

kalmoy *transitive verb* help

kamaoo retard, loco, mental

kamil 100 percent, full, perfect

kanees gay, homo

kanina or **kanin** pill

kanisa tabernacle

kanisad church

kanunioye hamming

kanuni mumble, hum

kanyag to smash or step on

kaqiro admit

kar card

karrabbo to put effort to get need

karbash whip

karbuna flashlight

karbuno flashlights

karamo magic

karamole magician

Kareem male name; generous

kazhe lunch

kazhe aanq eat lunch

kazheay have lunch

karri cook

karrioye cooking

karrisbook cookbook

karriy cooked

karenq lotion

karenqirri sunscreen

karetta wagon, carriage

karass nausea

karto clue

kashawita screw driver

kas purpose

kass to know, to get, to understand

kasse know

kassiy understood, got it

kassab force

kasso hope, to know

kassoye know

kassoyte *feminine* know

kasto every

kastumo boxer short

kattaar door latch

kattaar to latch

kattino cuff; handcuff

kattifad carpet

kattito zucchinis

kauaqai to make (something) to be at the end

kauinq unkind person, self-centered, egocentric; evil

kaun this

kawb to have

kawb not single, married

kawbte or **kawe** have, married to

kawo catch, seize

kawozha *plural* catch, seize

kawozhiy past tense of *khawo*

kawoub cold

kawoubis air conditioner

kawous shower, bath

kawouso take a shower; take a bath

kawouy to bathe

kayno our

kay my

kayiy hid

kee aharo anything, anyone

keelkeel risk

keel risk

kee the, the one, one of

kee it or thing

kee kau yours

kee kau wa it's yours

kee kay mine

kee kay wa it's mine

kee kayno ours

kee kayno wa it's ours

kee sheh hers, its, his

kee sho theirs

kee sho wa it is theirs

keli self, only

kelmad word

keydi to trick

keyh *masculine* which

keyh wa which is it

keyh wa usu which is he

kaihr peaceful, goodness

Khadija or **Khazhija** female name; premature

khafif light, not heavy

Khalif male name; successor

khall pestle

khamar gambling, gamble

khanq cheek

khanzeer senseless

Khamees Thursday

khasara disgraceful thing, unspeakable problem

khasarey a person who brings an unspeakable problem

khatarr incredible, genius

khus to pile up

ki variant of "you"

kintir clitoris

kingh *plura*l your

kirr an expression; "screw off" or scram

kissi bastard

kiawo wrench

kiawo'o the wrenches

kibwila bat

kish package, sack

kiuh to start (a machine)

kiuhinq trigger

kiuhis starting button; starter

kllabb tool, equipment

kobb shoe

kobb'o the shoes

kofia hat, cap

ko on, away, from, than

ko than (used to imply "rather than you," "rather than you guys")

ko on, on top (something)

ko from (used to imply "from you")

kokouris pet

konfur south

kol turn: an opportunity to do or use something before or after other people

kola glue

kombo can, the metal container that holds food or drink

kongfah cough

kongfahiy coughed

kongfol tree bark

konton fifty; 50

konton bogol five thousand; fifty hundred

konton kun fifty thousand

konton milyon fifty million

kool eyeliner

kool'o the eyeliners

koolo to eyeline self (depends on usage) or can be spelled out as *koolzho*

kooley-allamitta or **kooley-albanjarr** hedgehog

kooral recipe ingredient, recipe

koor to walk fast, fast

koori to make (something) walk fast

kop cup

kor up, top

korhorr upload

kormear to look after someone or something

koronto copper wire

korontosur outlet

korr climb

korrkorr to rape

korre climber

korrow monkey

korrow climber

kor shann high five

kouri to adopt, raise

kouris child support

kous group, individual as a group, family

kowanq slaughter house

kowe one

kowayd 1st, first

kouy come

kshalain alone, by self

kshenq bring

kshen *transitive verb* bring

kshena bring (referring to more than one)

ksheniy brought

kshentiy brought (referring to a female)

ku *plural* support the plural things that is not specific

kubbad *lexicon* "ball"

kuberto blanket

kulah used to express when "somthing" been said or done

kulai to heat (something) up, to twinge

kulazhiy got hot, got twinged

kulel hot

kulelis heater, microwave

kulaiti collar

kulli all

kullioun all the time, always

kullisho all of them

kumbay gizzard

kumoos vulva

kumunq main, meaningful

kumbo monsters

kun thousand

kuquto armpit

kurbo lots of stress and pressure

kurdtun *noun* log

kurdtun'o the logs

kuras chair

kurr plate with food

kursi seat

kursi dhifir seat belt

kus slice of (something), piece

kusar watery sauce

kush bush

kuur to be fast or hard

kuuri snore

kuwb spill, throw away

kuwiy past tense of of *kuwb*

kuwbtiy *feminine* past tense of *kuwb*

kwaun these

kwaas those

kwee *plural* the

kwee kau or **kwee nay** *plural* mine

kwee kau or **kwee nau** *plural* yours

kwee kayno *plural* ours

kwee sheh *plural* his, hers, its

kwee sho *plural* theirs, hers, its

kwee ningh *plural* yours *plural* (used when the owner is plural and the belonging is plural)

kyh to move, get out of, wake

kylli kidney

kyan betray

kyano betrayal

kyanole betrayer

L

laab to bend, corner, fold

laabinq to turn

laabje queasy

laan branch

la supposed to, a must, or what will happen

la "somebody is going to" or "somebody got"

labbis to dress, dress

labbiso get dressed up

ladhu dice

laf bone

laf'o bones

lahaw pain, hurt

lahash doofus

lagamo necessary

laih an expression of disappointment or sympathy

laiwitto yeasts

lakab extra teeth, supernumerary teeth

laking but

lakk lake

lalush bribe, payment

lalaab fold (used when there is more than one)

lalawb to touch multiple times

lami tar, sticky material that used for road surfaces

lamwadha between, center

lamwa two, bi, 2

lamwa bogol two hundred

lamwa dhini two sides

lamwa gour two times

lamwa jair two times

lamwa kun two thousand

lamwa marr two times

lamwa milyon two thousand

lamwazho couple

lamwayd second, 2nd

landhu a square designed game that played with one dice

lanq clitoris hood

lazhir villain, antagonist

lastiko elastic

lauab toy

lauag fund, money

lauala in case

lauan without, lack

lawb touch

lawblawbo nauseous

lawiy touched

lawatan twenty, 20

lawe lack, less

lawoy to guess

lawoyiy *masculine* guessed

lawoytiy guessed

lawwanq *lexicon* "cream"

library library

le only, just

leesh aim

lehe own, belong

lehen owner

lef lick

lefto cream

lenq lane

lewaa got to, should

leyr fresh air

lhauang an expression; "seriously"

liki used to express on (something) that's happening or happened

lillahi a very nice, merciful and rightful person

lima ness, as

leemo orange, grapefruit

leemo bambele grapefruit

leemo dhanaw lime, lemon

liin lime, lemon

liwah lion

looghun express: acts of problem on neck or to be burden on the neck

loogad language

loomina acoustic

lor a sack that is made out of plastic strength

lous peanut

louy cow

louygaissi buffalo

lugg foot

lugg'o the feet

luggoy to travel by feet, walk

luglugo gargle

lujad accent

lumi forfeit, lose

lume loser

luqajhenda iguana

luug curve, corner

luul pearl

luwi or **nyauwmalay** catfish

lxa to owe

lxahe owe

lxahayiy past tense of *lxahe*

lxe six, hexa

lxehayd sixth, 6th

lxehayiy past tense of *lxehe*

lxehe stain

lxeheran sixty

lxegais hexagon

M

ma mom, ma

maa which, where, what or what kind of (used in reverse way, especially compared with English)

maal treasure

Maalmadon the fourth month

Maanti today

maanto mythological story or bedtime story

maarsa static, electric

maarsa qaloon electric eel

maari to put on or rub on

maay the most used expression in Mai-Mai world; "Of course," "For what?" "Why not?" "What's up?" ought, presuppose

maar copper

madama *lexicon* "as", "because", or "since"

macg intend

macgall lexicon: listen

Maddhurow male name, means "a person who like to save money or something"

magal shelf

maghala town

maghar skin, leather

maghas scissor

maga name

magalawe nameless

magrib evening, evening prayer

magribcui to be obvious or having connection toward the prayer of evening

mau not, won't (used before a verb)

mau ahay nea was not

mahaboos prison

mahaboosle prisoner

mahad sacred, hollowed, revered, saint, great

mahadsin grateful, wonderful, kind

mahadsinte "you are kind"

maharifa kindness, generosity

mahhkama court

mahl none, un, no, nobody, nothing

mahle not appear to be, not exist

mahle without, less

mahlrawo unwanted

mahmaho riddle

majar to envy

majarso envy

mauquure stingy

maunahe a person who doesn't hasitate to do bad thing

maigailed masculine

maigail male

maigail sahib male friend

maighain protective or ensures a safe environment, to be under protection

maighain Allah "God, have mercy"; to seek God's protection

mai what, why

Mai-Mai the most common and the native language in Somalia

Mai-Mai the language of expression

maigaid leather

maihyrr money or property to give to spouse when a wife and husband getting marry; kind of like dowry

mairjhi to chock; throttle; strangle

mairqo get chock

masra stage

majar to brag achievement to hurt other's feeling

majhuji squeeze

makhaya restaurant

makeena machine

makharin fishing hook

maktab *lexicon* "library"

malmal myrrh

mala pus

malab honey

malabwey *feminine* honey, darling

malacg death wish

malacgkamoaid *noun* doom, death

malan day

malan tzaun this day; today

malan kasto every day

malansamel daylight, daytime

malaria malaria

malawow honey, darling

maley fish

maleyhindig starfish

malailig brain

malauig angel

malehe suppose, might, reckon

Malik male name; master

mama mommy, mom

mamil customer

mamud thumb

mamul manage

mamule manager

mamuley *feminine* manager

mamulow *masculine* manager

manasooa a child or teenage that is cursed

mananjir bachelor; a man who is not married (age from eighteen up)

mandhyrr intestine

mannq hero, bold

mann feminine of *mannq*

mantag vomit, puke

mantagiy past tense of *mantag*

manyag soft

manyagmanyag way soft, very soft

maqan *noun* absence

maqanye absent, missing

maqante *feminine* absent, missing

mar to pass, go, or come through; to step or ride on (something)

maracg soup

Mareka America, USA

Marekan American

mariy past tense of *mar*

marka so, then, furthermore

markab cargo, ship

markhati witness

marmar to pass over and over, many times

marmariy past tense of *marmar*

marouji twist

marr moment, time

marr dambe next time or other time

marr kaas that time

marr kalle other time

marr kasto every time

marr quo once, some time

marrmarr from time to time

marrmarr quo from time to time, some time

marsho gear

marwo ma'am

marti visitor, guest

marti'o the visitors

malwah Somali pancake

mariid venom, or something look or feel rough

mas serpent

masasa plastic bottle

masakeen poor, pity

masajid mosque

masaruf money that a housewife uses to take care of the needs of a household

masewyr picture

mashi a friend's wife or husband or brother-in-law or sister-in-law; short for "dumashi"

mashqul busy

masha Allah congratulation; "God (Allah) has willed it"

mauassia the act of adultery and fornication (*zina*)

masqarad mask

masquur helpless

masseer jealous, jealousy

masseertiy past tense of *masseer*

mastarada ruler, measurer

matanyo twin

matanyo'o the twins

matha head

mathaweyna president

mattour engine, motor

maudo or maud condition, to allow on condition

mauqul reasonable, good reason

mauadanq silver

mauana meaning, because, mean

mauanamahle meaningless

mauana sheh its meaning

mauanoy to make (someone or something) a big deal

maxaa *lexicon* "what"

maul to milk

maualgo teaspoon

maualinq master or teacher (mostly referring to a Islamic religious teacher)

mauam deal

mauh sweet, kiss, pleasant

mauhsalam "Goodbye."

mauarad enemy

mauackante *lexicon* know

maweelo entertainment

maweel entertain

mawgg for nothing

mawlaf to empty

maxqan intellect, brain

mayondo ape

mayya no

mayyanqmayyanq dessert, sweet food

mayyan sweet

mazhow black

mazhow alen or **alen mazhow** black tea

mazhow biyo or **biyo mazhow** black water

mazhow goud or **goud mazhow** black hole

mazhow karamo black magic

mazhow il or **il mazhow** black eye

mazhow baraf or **baraf mazhow** black ice

mazhul charcoal

meeg rocket

meeg'o the rockets

mega how much, how many

mega habad how many

meer drain

mees table, desk

mehe not, is not

meheto isn't, it isn't, not (used with "you")

mehetona *plural* aren't (used with "you guys")

meheyo isn't, it isn't, not

meheno *plural* it isn't, isn't (used with "us")

meheyona aren't, not (used with "they")

meyl place, somewhere, area

meyltzo or **meyl'uo** somewhere, where

Meyleechore the fifth month

Meyleedambe the sixth month

mid *lexicon* "thing" or "same thing"

midab *lexicon* "color"

milyon million

milyone millionaire

minna sperm, cum

mindi knife

minink house

mininkhaas housewife

minshar saw, handsaw

mir cerebrum, mind

mirigg vanish, dematerialize

mithig right position

mis whether, or

miskalle otherwise, or

missar ax

missir lentil

mitir meter

miya *lexicon* is it, does it

mizanq scale

moaid corpse, dead body

Mohammed variant of *Muhammad*; highly praiseworthy

mohog waist

mol deep

monq big, giant

monqfoore big fool

moro range

morouthi elephant

mos banana

moto motorcycle

mourdi wheat

Mowlid third month

mouy mortar, the one used with pestle

mouzhd to cross, to pass

mouzhdti to let (something or someone) pass

mubarak blessed, happy

mudd assume, think

muddo decision

muddsan famous, well-known

mufo a round and flat baked Somali bread

Muhammad male name; the highly praiseworthy

mugo an expression; "for real"

mugdi dark

muheem important

muheem wa it's important

mukulal a male cat

Mumina female name; believer

Mumin short for *Mumina*

Muminey female name; religiously faithful

munyug newborn, infant

munyug yal newborns

munyug'o the newborns

muqda evidence

mushar wage, salary

musqul restroom

mustaqbal important thing or need, future

mulimuli tadpole

murah seed

murah'o the seeds

moorat *noun* needy or need

murka sprain

muroog stress, tension

murooji *transitive verb* stress; to make (someone) stress

murr variant of *clitoris*

murug muscular, musculature

murugle muscular person, body builder

murun argue

musba small lamp

musharario porridge

musib sad, tragic

musika music

Muslima female name; a Muslim woman

Muslunq Muslim

musqul maigailed male restroom or men's room

musqul bilamed female restroom or ladies' room

muso to smirk

musmar nail, screw

musugmusug or **musug** to get (somebody) mad or nerve

muthan sir

mutoor urethra

muurey female ape

muwaraka gift, holiday freebie

muwata duck

N

na used in plural

naa how or what about, and

naag woman

naag'o the women

naar hell

nabwi prophet

nabwi Isa Prophet Isa, Jesus

nabwi Muhammad Prophet Mohammed

nap a sticky thing that made of elastic, stucky thing

nacg to take (something) back, again or repeat

nacgnolasho reincarnation

nacgo go back, return

nacgizhiy went back

nacgitiy *feminine* went back

naf soul, life, self

nafaqo nourishment; nutrition

nafas space

naftika directly to second person

nafto fuel

nah startle, to show care

naharis to be kind or care; to show mercy

nahi to make someone startled

nahyiy past of *nahi*

nahiy past tense of *nah*

nahtiy *feminine* past tense of *nah*

nahas pot

nakata expression: "forcely refused"

nar groan, moan

naibwaid peace, wonderful

naibwaidgailio farewell

naiwyrr time, chance

naiwyrr *noun* physical tension

nall lightbulb

nambaro numbers

namus self-control, discipline

nanna candy

nanna suuf cotton candy

nanna yal candies

nanis or **nanismaga** nickname

narjinq coconut

nas breast, nipple

nasib luck

nasibsinte lucky

nasiblow a lucky person

nasiiri kindergarten

nasrereb bra

nathir rare

nathif clean good, clean

nathifa a female name; clean

nathifi to clean (something) good

nathifyiy past tense of *nazhifi*

nauas moron

nauam yes

nau your (used when there is more than one)

nauc hate

naucala *noun* burden, hate

nauctiy *feminine* hated

nauciy hated

nawb accuse

nawbtiy *feminine* accused

nawiy accused

nawooji to tie tightly

naya you girl, girl

nazhi announcement; announce

nea didn't, not (used with "mau")

neaf livestock a live goat, chicken, cow

nef sigh, breath, air

nefdhow to breathe in and out

nefkuur to breathe hard or fast

nefso to catch breath, breathe

neftoor breathe out, exhale

nefqazhd breathe in, inhale

neb diaper

neng should had, did (used backward)

niey *feminine* mate

ni ken let's go

ni kena let's all go

nep to rest

nepso rest

nha tasteful, valuable

ni variant of "us"

niid heart and mind

nikka engagement, to get engaged

niyad spirit

nijiss unpure or disguting (noun)

niow bro, mate

niqab a veil worn by Muslim women

niqis pantie

Mai-Mai (Somali) Dictionary

niqis'o the panties

no *plural* from, on, off, than, away (used with "us")

no on, to be on top of (something) (used with "us")

no from (used to imply "from us")

no than (used to imply "rather than us")

nogo become, be

nogizhiy became

nogitiy *feminine* became

nola or **nolosho** life

nol to be alive, life

nolaw be alive, live

noldon ghost

nole alive

nolnol creature

nolnol'o the creatures

nolnol badd or **badd nolnol** sea creature

nolnolbiyo amphibian

noag tire, to become weary

noagiy past tense of *nog*

noagman tiredness

noono slang word for "baby"

noor colorful, shine

noor color

Noor male name; shine

noa color, version

noa yal plural of *noa*

nuglai to make (something) weak or flexible, loosen up

nul shake

nulnul to shake multiple time

number number

number'o the numbers

nunuug pacifier

nus or **barr** half

nuug to suck

nyaanya tomato

nyaanya yal tomatoes

nyamo flesh, meat

nyamuto anus

nyanyur kitty cat, kitten

nyauw cat

nyif nip

nyirif pinch

nyirifiy pinched

nyiriftiy *feminine* pinched

nynko like, act like

nyn person, somebody, someone

nynq masculine of *nyn*

nynba nobody

nyn bauh everyone

nyn yal plural of nyn

nynq quo some man, a man

nynkasto everybody, everyone

nyukis *noun* twerk

nyuki twerk, to shake own butt

O

o away, on, off, from, than (used with "me")

o than, rather than

o on, on top of (something) (used with "me")

o from; "from me"

oa of, that, around

oa *adjective* that

odso request, order

ozhd to close

ozhiy closed

ogolasho permission

ogolaw to accept (something)

okialo glasses

okialoindho eyeglasses

okialoirri sunglasses

oll when two people stop talking to each other because they are mad each other or they are no longer friends.

ood bar

oolumo priest

oomul postpartum, confinement

oomulis midwife or nurse

oma feminine of *omo*

omo ground soap; soap powder

Omur male name; gifted to lead

onq thirst

oniy *masculine* got thirsty

ontiy got thirsty

oonq or **oom** *noun* smoke, fume

oor stomach

oormariid purely evil

oos hush, zip

orod *lexicon* "run"

oronjo juice

orsad bear

osbo salt

othi a male senior

ou *lexicon* "or"

oulad *lexicon* "child"

Ouji called by one of Somali tribes, it means "Enjoy today tomorrow is not promised", it's simulated with Italian word OGGI which means "today".

ouyi to make (someone) cry

ouy cry

ouyiy cried

ouytiy *feminine* cried

owri two or more women who married to a one man, one man's wives, the wives of one man

owri dislike, referring to people who have issues among themselves

owthow enemy, evil

owg to notice, realize, aware

owgaisiys warning

owgaso notice

owgaw aware

owgsinte *feminine* aware

owrr cloth

owrroye clothing

P

phel file

pheyr fist, knuckle

phili expect

philink television

philin'o the television

pimbais gray

Q

qaal basta fork

qaal farrkaiti fork

qaal maualga spoon

qaal monq big spoon

qaal spoon

qaar some

qad a black ink that is made of charcoal

qafis cage

qaib to share, part, dividend

qaibiow divider

qaibso share

qaimaithi barley

qal surgery

qalab luggage

qalaf shelf

qaloon eel

qalman operation; surgery

qalad incorrect, wrong

qalanq pen, pencil

qalanq gaid pencil

qalanq ampira pen

qalanq maga pen name

qaley to excuse mischief, or forgiver

Qamar female name; moon

qamri alcohol, liquor

qanniin bite

qandho fever

qanjar melon

qanjarif scratch, pinch

qansal cancel

qamees a long full-length loose-fitting robe worn by sheikhs or some Muslim men (dishdash)

qar can, able to do

qarol fruit

qarauh to blow up

qarauhiy exploded

qarauhsi to blow (something) up

qareeb outlander

qareemad attorney

qarfaid ajar

qari to hide, not to tell

qarr *lexicon* "hot"

qarrqarr very hot

qas bladder

qash terrible, very bad, unpleasant

qashag messy, trashy

qashagoy to make messy

qashagqashag very trashy

qashyn trash, litter

qashyn qub trash can

qasab sugarcane

qattar danger

qattarbir bulldozer

qatina necklace

qayli to yell, scream, make noise

qawal to rush, to go or be fast

qeweshdhow to jerk off, to masturbate

qabwil clan

qazhd take, pick

qazhda something that picks something, picker, spoon

qazhiy picked

qaweer old or big

qias to make average

qharer bitter, embitter

qhass to pour water in or mix with water, to mess or wet with water, the way to make dough

qhali expensive

qhor neck

qhorsaghare headlock

qhortahg lizard

qhortahgo lizards

quo *masculine* some, a (ajective)

qodax *lexicon* "thorn"

qoaminye not wanting to do something

qoazhd speak

qoazhoye speaking

qodob bill

qof one; person; body

qof quo someone, body, person

qof tzo *feminine* someone, person, body

qofyey a female person; miss

qofyow a male person; mister

qoffon coffin

qoho crew, team

qohouti refugee

qol room

qoolley *lexicon* "dove"

qolkawous bathroom

qolof shell, cover

qolsarir bedroom

qolwaihyll roommate

qoobb the sound of knock

qoobbqoobb the sound of knocks

qoobbdhow knock

qoodha or **ka dhi** a gesture of using hand to slap someone's hand to show thrill about accomplishment, to give five

qool leash

qoomi penny

qoonto butt, ass

qor write

qoraal script

qorey writer

qori gun

qoroto carrot

qorr body

qorrax *lexicon* sun

qorraxley *lexicon* "sunshine or beautiful"

qorri piece of firewood

qorrnyo firewoods

qoshol laugh, funny

qosholow laugher

qosholis comedian

qouri flirt

qoyli vagina

qoy to wet

qouys group

qozhd dig

qrrau watermelon

qub husk, the outer covering

qudqudto *noun* tickles

qudqudtoy to tickle

quff fall down; trip

qural recipe

quful lock, to lock

quraac *lexicon* "breakfast"

quraac aanq eat breakfast

quraaco have breakfast

qural vegetable

qural jinni fungus

Quran Quran

qurun thorn

Quttab Bible (mostly referring to the Quran)

Quttab Jama or **Jama Quttab** Holy Bible

quur to give, to give up

R

raaho pleasure, enjoyment

raathi to look for, seek, search

rabben tame

rabi lord

raggay tamarind

ragh toad

rafazhd struggle, plight

rafazhiy struggled

rah to follow, to go with

rahan herd

rahiy past tense of *rah*

Raheem (Arabic) creator of mankind; "God gives mercy to his believers"

Rahman (Arabic) creator of mankind; merciful

Rahma (Arabic) God; most merciful

rai testicle

rai'o the testicle

rajail favorite

rajeay wish

raig man

raig'o the men

rakka form of prostration done in Islamic prayer

rali apology

raligaili or **raliyel** apologize

ralihahaw sorry

ramol trailer

ramud remote, remote control

ranji ink, paint

rama lava

raqa frog

ragees cheap

raseed receipt

raseay pack

rashin grocery

rashin'o the groceries

rabsho trouble

rabshole trouble maker

rasas meg, pack of bullets

rather sense

rathio radio

rarasi wash out, rinse

rasi rinse

rasool a messenger that is very close to God

rasool Allah messenger of God

rawb want

rewb to stop, prevent, or block

rewiy past tense of *rewb*

rerewb to prevent continually

rih press, click

rihiy past tense of *rih*

rhehr group of people who live together and have something in common

rhid drop; to drop (something)

rhob rain

rhobdhi rainfall

rhobdhioye rainfalling, "it is rain"

rhoboye "it's raining"

rhob kuwoye rain spilling, rain dropping, "it's raining"

rhobrhid raindrop

rhorr to load, to put on

rhorriy past tense of *rhorr*

rhoug rape

riff scar

riwaayad entertainment

riyo fantasy or dream

ron to be better, should

ronye better

ronte better (referring to a female)

ror run

rora *plural* run

rorow runner

roug mat

rouri supply truck

routi bread

rouy win

rumo toothbrush

rumoy to brush teeth

rungh true

rungh wa it's true

runn truth, right

runn tzee wa it's the truth

ruux person

ruux'o the persons

S

sa let's, from where at, from

saafi pure and clear

saag to move on surface smoothly

saan footstep

saaranq tray

saar to put on

saariy past tense of *saar*

saas like that

saas wa that's it, it's like that

sa bah let's go

sa baha let's go (used when there is more than one person)

sa bahro the act of studying or learning

sabun soap

saboorad board

sacgeer small or little one

sauc calf

sadaqa alms, almsgiving, charity

Sadik male name; truthful

sa dhaf leave, to leave (something or someone) behind

sa dhiib handover

sadhowazha *plural* welcome, come closer

sadhowaw welcome, come closer

Saeed or **Saiid** male name; happy

Saf to line (something) up

safaleeti *lexicon* "woman scarf"

Safar the second month

safar journey

safar period of time

sa gal come in

sa gaili to bring (something or someone) in

saghal nine, nona

sagharre hare

sah to sign, to correct, to check

sahi signature, sign

sahiy past of *sah*

sahihiy past tense of *sahi*

sahanq plate

sahariir torment

sahib friend

sahib bilan female friend

sahibgaiwyrr or **gaiwyrrsahib** girlfriend

sahib maigail or **maigailsahib** male friend

Saibti Saturday

saidyh three; tri; 3

saidyhayd third

saidyh bogol three hundred

saidyh dhini three sides

saidyhgais triangle

saidyh gour three times

saidyh jair three times

saidyh kun three thousand

saidyh marr three times

saidyh milyon three million

saidyhayd third

saitun guava

saitun yal guavas

saitun'o the guavas

sajood is in the middle of upper forehead

sa kyh wake up, get up

sa kyhi to wake (somebody) up

sa kyhiy woke up

saghal dhini nine side

saghalayd ninth, 9th

saghal gais nine angles, nonagon

saghalshan ninety

saghalshan dhini ninety side

saghalshan gais ninety angles

saqin blade, razor blade

sa kawo to go catch (something or someone)

sal base

salaahi to rub softly, rub

Salah male name; prayer

salahd the five pillars of Islam (*salat*)

salahd'o the prayers

salahd yal prayers

salbloun baseball

salhos basement

salaho slide

salauampira or **fiondo** slingshot

salan or **salam** greet

saldhig *lexicon* "station"

salli prayer rug

Salat male name; prayer

salatta lettuce

salboqo bean

salboqo malauey string bean

salboqo girgir pinto bean

salboqo kylli kidney bean

salid oil

salid hunggur food oil

salid jiffi lard

salmad eulogy

sa korr come up, come on, get on

samath welkin, the upper atmosphere

sambab lung

samboob hood, the hood of car

sambusa Somali samosa

sameay make; invent

samiid concrete

samme credit, point

samme kar credit card

sana year

sanabook yearbook

sa nacg bring back

sa nacgiy brought back

sa nacgizhiy came back

sa nacgo come back

sandoog casket

sandoog'o the caskets

sanq nose

sanq bor running nose

sanjaweel ginger

sanood ready money, cash

saqarad about to die; close to die

sar skyscraper

saraf change, to make (something) into decimal or multiple ways, decimal change

sareen rye

sarr cut

sarir bed

sarirwaqti bedtime

sarir biyo water bed

sawb or **sasawb** allure

sasawiy allured

sakatta crocodile

saua clock, time

sauad watch, timer

Sauabi *lexicon* "clap"

sauh hour, o'clock

sauh time

saun like this

saun wa it's like this

sawb entice

sawiy enticed

sa waayiy couldn't find

sawab reason

sawar to forgive

sawouti escort; the act of accompanying (someone or something) the way out or halfway to his/her destination/transportation, kind of like escort.

sai spouse

sayyu female's sister-in-law

sbital hospital

seexo *lexicon* "lie down"

seaw go to, get to or to be (somewhere)

seazhiy went

seeb to yank, to remove

seenq snot

seenia big and rounded food plate

sef machete

sefdhuub sword

sei how, way, proper, highly, as, very, why, or what

sei kalle *adverb* other way, opposite (usually used when things having differences)

sinebdazhd waking up in the middle of sleep

seithyy how (used in questions a lot)

sei tzaas wa that is how

sei tzaun wa this is how

sei tzee the way

seiwais *noun* jerk off

seiwaiso jerk off; masterbate

seuho to choke on (something)

sewyr depiction, image

seydi male's brother-in-law

sey and them

sgaiddis dump truck

shaay sweet tea

shab a rounded game played by girls

shabdhow or **anshabdhow** clap

shaf trim

shaffela driver's partner

shagaf roof

shahazhd to get (something) from (someone) in smooth way

shahid onlooker, eyewitness, witness

shahaado diploma, degree

shairqan sewing machine

shaitan devil, Satan

sharero traditional Somali Bantu music and dance

shaki suspect, doubt

shal bihi to separate

shal goysozha partake, share

shal goy to make (something) into parts or pieces, divide

shaley yesterday

shamad floor, the bottom of area

shamendo cement

shallaay regret

shalqaibi divid

shambar Somali ancestor

shambar'o the original Somali ancestors, they usually have firm hair

shambyrri always

shamunq attack

shamuma *plural* attack

shamanq whisker

shando *lexicon* "casket"

shann five; penta; 5

shannayd fifth

shann bogol five hundred

shann dhini five side

shann gour five times

shann jair five times

shanema movie theater

shanngais pentagon

shann kun five thousand

shangle small plastic container

shanle comb

Shanleay to comb (hair)

shann milyon five million

shannto few

shann tzee shambar the five Somali ancestors, also known as the five Ms; they are Makua, Majindou, Manyasa, Millima, and Manyawou

shaqqale worker

shaqqe work, job

shaqqeayoye working

shaqqe lauan without job

shaqqelawe jobless

shaqqeay to work, work

shaqqeye employer

shaqsi to be on self

sharra decorate

sharabb try

sharadd bet

sharara violin

sharaf respect

shar bad thing, evil

sharsoobiow or **sharfale** evildoer

sharamuto whore, bitch

shari law

sharile lawyer

shariole attorney

shashad screen

shati T-shirt

Shauaban the eighth month

shawaqa net

shawail tiger

shela testicle or a sickness that grows testicles big and with result of pain

sheli mono

sheg tell

shegiy told

shego choose, decide

shegizhiy chose

shegitiy *feminine* chose

shegtiy *feminine* told

sheh his, its, her

sheer reek

sheezhd ground, to crush (something) into very small pieces; grind

sheezhiy past tense of *sheezhd*

sheikh a leader of Muslims, Muslim role model, preacher

sheka conversation, story, narrative

shekasheka story

shey stuff, thing

shi shy, to be ashamed

shyiy past of *shi*

shiil fry

shiil'o the fries

shiid *noun* rock

shiid yal rocks

shiish target

shikshig stutter

shikshigow a stuttering person

shirika when something owned by more than one person; share

shishi shy

shinni bee

shimbir bird

shinoli toilet

shinyeri zipper

shirkad corporation

shir conference

shirif pick comb

shitto vagina, pussy

shizhd to turn on, to set on (fire)

shizhiy past tense of *shizhd*

sholonshol *noun/verb* to fry meat with its fat or with food oil

shob to dress nice, classy, classic

shobar chipmunk

shob to dress nice

shobshob gloat

sho their

shol comedy

sholad chimney

shoob pour

shoonq pubes, pubic hair

shorobo med syrups

shouri whisper

show commercial, advertise or show

showiste a person who likes to show off

shraab alcohol drink

shub to quiet

shub dheh be quiet

shuf penis

shufto bandit

shufto yal bandits

shughul duty, work, job

shukami to flirt

shukuman towel

shukul thrash

shumi to give a kiss

shumis *noun* kiss

shumauh candle

shuma kiss (referring to more than one)

shunq or **shum** kiss

shupp pile, to pile up

shuqul to beat (someone or something)

shuwunq diarrhea

siasa clue, plan, idea, or trick

sidaid eight, octa

sidaidayd eighth, 8th

sidaid dhini eight side

sidaidtan eighty

sidaid gais eight angles, octagon

Sieaital the eleventh month

sigouni private

Siid long blouse that Somalian women wear

Siil cunt

sigar cigarette

sig to miss from danger

sithi since, ever since

sirr trick, secret

sin or **si** variant of "you guys"

sihir voodoo, hex

sihirole voodooist, voodoo doer

silig chain-link fence, wire fence

silsila necklace, chain

silsilad chain

singsigar lighter, cigarette lighter

siyman gift

sisin sesame

sitimanq week

siwo dust

siwaidd continue

siy give, pay, feed

siyiy past tense of *siy*

siyn tip

skasho sock

skasho'o the socks

Skool School

Skoolay scholar, student

so *plural* from, on, off, than, away (used with "you guys")

soco *lexicon* "walk"

soddon thirty, 30

soddon bogol three thousand; thirty hundred

soddon kun thirty thousand

soddon milyon thirty million

soddo father-in-law

sofiid attic

soafa sharpener

sor polenta, grits

sol sex

solota couch

soloto couches

somo namesake, when two or more people have the same name

Somou *jillauh*, the Somali clan that have soft hair

somow or **somhe** a person who fasts all the time without eating and drinking

Songh the ninth month, the month of fasting (Ramadan)

Songhfurr the tenth month, the month of the opening or no more Ramadan

somiy fasted

sonqtiy *feminine* fasted

sonq to fast, to not eat or drink

soobi fix; do, make

soobyiy past of *soobi*

soofi a religious person

soobcua early morning, before dawn, morning prayer (*fajr*)

soobcui to be obvious or having connection toward the prayer of morning

sooh faint

soohiy fainted

soohtiy *feminine* fainted

soonq or **soal** sharp

soor hang

staishinq station

staishinq bas bus station

soqqor sugar

soqqorow diabetes

starasha hankerchief

stimi to warmly enjoy

stiuimal use

stiuimaliy used

subhana Allah (Arabic) "Oh my god."

suaal question

sug wait, await

sugiy awaited, waited

sugey waitress

sugow waiter

suhoor the last meal of the day for a fasting person and have to be done before sunrise; before sunrise meal

sul toe

sul'o the toes

sulgoy both crab and lobster

sultan sultan (pronounced slightly different from English)

sunn poison, acid

sunn battaria or **battaria ashita** battery acid

sur to hang or input (something)

surunq "freeze" or "stand"

surad beauty

surad a chapter in the Quran

sutto sense

sutto gal make sense

surwal pan

surwal jaimis jean pan

suuf cotton

suunq belt, seatbelt

suugo sauce

suwug butter

suwug uano or **uano garour** butter milk

suwug lefto butter cream

syrim to slip

syrimbi singular of *syrimbo*

syrimbizhiy slipped

syrimbitiy *feminine* slipped

syrimbisyrimbi slippery

syrimbo *noun* slip

T

taar telephone

tabo dial, touch

tacg *lexicon* "move" or "go"

taf leg

taf'o the legs

tafaliqow flip, back flip, front flip

tageer fan, support

tahalil holy water

taisi housefly

tajir rich

talab step

talab'o the steps

talabso to step or walk through over (something)

tali to make a plan, dictate, plan

Taliani Italian

talal injection, vaccine

Talaatha Tuesday

talulia tornado

tamar energy

tapp idea

tappela billboard

tappepa a piece of cloth put around head, head wrap

taqtaari to prepare (something or someone)

taqtaaryiy past tense of *taqtaari*

taqtaaritiy *feminine* past of *taqtaari*

taqtar doctor

taqtarad nurse

tarr to be useful, effective

tarara to slip or slide

tareeg rend, tear

tareegiy past tense of *tareeg*

tariikh date; period; time; month, day, and year

tarmush tea flask, thermos

taracg match: a chemically prepared wick used in firing powder

tarenq train, the vehicle

tartanq race, tournament

tarteeb slow

tarteebqo Slowly

tas *noun* drip

tasal drip

tasaliy past tense of tasal

tasaloye dripping

tattombeay to hit heavily or hard in the back of (somone)

tattombo noun of *tattombeay*

taualin education

tauasio funeral

tawo fry pan

tawabahr training

tawb to leave or to leave (something or someone) behind

tawiy past tense of *tawb*

tawwar muscle, energy

taxathir careful

taxg to raise (hands or something), to stretch

taxgiy past tense of *taxg*

taxi taxi

taxile taxi driver

tchunju coop, chicken house

tchunju doro chicken coop

tead a huge fence or boundary around houses that keeps dangerous animals away

teer lean

teerso to lean

tenda tent

tex text

texiy texted

teyh *feminine* which

teyh wa eeh which is she

tif toothpick

tifig leak

tifigoye leaking

tihir or **tihiri** variant of "maggot"

tiir pillar

tiitinq cactus

tilmanq point

tilmamiy pointed

timir'o the dates

tinaar oven

tin hair

tin hargag nappy hair

trii to count, count down

tryiy past tense of *trii*

tir delete, erase

tiriy past tense of *tir*

tirenq eraser

tirri *lexicon* "say" or "said"

tirtir wipe

tirtiriy wiped

tirtirenq wiper

tis bit

tis tzo little bit

tiwff to skin

tomwon ten, deca tomwon

tomwonayd tenth; 10th

tomwon dhini ten sides

tomwon gais ten angles, decagon

tomwon iyo kowe eleven

tomwon kowayd eleventh; 11th

tomwon kowe dhini eleven sides

tomwon iyo kowe gais eleven angles, hendecagon

tomwon iyo lamwa twelve

tomwon iyo lamwa dhini twelve sides

tomwon iyo lamwa gais twelve angles, dodecagon

tomwon iyo saidyh thirteen

tomwon iyo saidyh dhini thirteen sides

tomwon iyo saidyh gaise thirteen angles

tomwon iyo affar fourteen

tomwon iyo affar dhini fourteen sides

tomwon iyo affar gais fourteen angles

tomwon iyo shann fifteen

tomwon iyo shann dhini fifteen sides

tomwon iyo shann gais fifteen angles

tomwon iyo lhe sixteen

tomwon iyo lhe dhini sixteen sides

tomwon iyo lhe gais sixteen angles

tomwon iyo tothowa seventeen

tomwon iyo tothowa dhini seventeen sides

tomwon iyo tothowa gais seventeen angles

tomwon iyo sidaid eighteen

tomwon iyo sidaid dhini eighteen sides

tomwon iyo sidaid gais eighteen angles

tomwon iyo saghal nineteen

tomwon iyo saghal dhini nineteen sides

tomwon iyo saghal gais nineteen angles

toash torch

tobo *noun* wining point

tohl supporting group, relative, community

tol sew, suture

toog beg

toogiy begged

toogow beggar

toonq garlic

toon'o the garlics

toor to pour (some heavy, thick, or hard stuffs) out, shoot, toss

toasi straighten, guide, fix, ajust

toasyiy past tense of *toasi*

toobo hose

toqo turn, to use something after or before

toqo chance

toqobiltoqo a Mai-Mai saying; "Everybody has his/her turn"; karma

toqotoqo turn by turn

torey dagger

tothowa seven, sept

tothowa dhini seven sides

tothowa gais seven angles, heptagon

tothowatan seventy

tothowatan dhini seventy sides

tothowatan gais seventy angles

tothowayd seventh, 7th

thruus straight or going straight

tow to be need something or someone

towiy past of *tow*

tubbo glass bottles

tuf spit

tuffa apple

tuffal pear

tukulish squirrel

tumiy past tense of *tung*

tunq or **tum** beat

tus *noun* show

tusi to show

tusale example

tusale ahan or **ahan tusale** for example

tush dot

tushtush chickenpox

tusyiy showed

tusitiy *feminine* showed

tusug bedraggle

tusugoy to make (something) bedraggle

tusugoyiy *masculine* past tense of *tusug*

tusugoytiy past tense of *tusug*

tusugowiy bedraggled

turjuman translate, translator

turturi to overcook

turturiy overcooked

turub game of cards; cards

tuug thief

tuug'o the thieves

tuur hump

tuwako tobacco

tzaas *feminine* that

tzau *feminine* your

tzaun *feminine* this or her

tzayno *feminine* our

tzay *feminine* my

tzee *feminine* the, the one

tzee *feminine* it or thing

tzeeahato *feminine* anything, anyone

tzee tzay *feminine* mine

tee tzau *feminine* yours

tzee tzayno *feminine* ours

tzee tzis *feminine* his, its

tzee tzio *feminine* theirs

tzo *feminine* some, a

U

uaay cuss, insult, dis

uaaytin cuss, cussing

uag plastic or something made of plastic

uag yal plural of *uag*

uaggte *feminine* look like

uaggye look like

uai who

ualangcual whine

uama when (usually used in questions)

uano milk

uano nul milk shake

uano nuug milk bottle

uanonas pineapple

uanonas yal pineapples

uamama a man scarf worn by Muslim man

uamano to give something to someone to hold it for protection or defences

uascuass to interrupt, to ruin, to mess up, to butt in

uayy booby trap, trap

uawai where

uawowa grandchild

ueeg push

ueegiy pushed

ueethyn army

uff disgusting

ugool grudge

uilif pole

uilla until, up to

uin ones, rest, whole

uin tzee kalle the other ones, the rest

uin tzaun this much, these ones

uin tzaun "this is it" or "that is all"

uin tzaun tanye this big

uin tzaas that much, those ones

uin tzaas "that is it" or "that is all"

uiptila disaster, troublesome

ukathi *lexicon* "wait"

ukun egg

ukun'o the eggs

ul stick

ultum ending, final, ultimate

uloos heavy, weight

umbar sweater

umri lifetime

umudd mankind

unsoor laziness

unsoore lazy

ultum ending, final, ultimate

unu us, we

unu abakayno ourselves

unugu *lexicon* "we" or "us"

ur smell, stink

urud firstborn child

uss get, pick, take

ussuu an expression of curiosity

usu him, he, it

usu abasheh himself

usub new

usub'o the news

usubkouyow newcomer

usuboqol newsroom

usugu *lexicon* "him", "he", "it"

uunq or **uum** to create (something) powerfully

uur pregnant

uus gut, belly

uusey abdomen, gut

uzhoy to poop

uzhoo poop

uzhoogalenq waste system, digestive system

uzhoogarangariow beetle

uzhur disease

W

wa it's, it is

wa right position

waa is it

waar beach

waar arra beach sand

waas those (used with nouns)

waaxe *lexicon* "it is"

waayahayy alright

waay to fail or say couldn't find (someone or something)

waayiy couldn't find (something or someone)

waaytiy to say she or you couldn't find (something or someone)

wacx item, material, substance

wacxaun expression: this thing

wadda path

wajip responsible, ought, have to

wajirra porn

wa kaay right there (*he's right there*)

wa kou right here (*he's right here*)

walin mental, insane

wa alaikum assalam (Arabic) salutation response: and upon you be peace

wadarr sum; total

wadda path, way

waddan nation

wa naay *plural* right there

wa nou *plural* right here

wa taay *feminine* right there

wattariri poison ant

wahrdi guard, secure

wahrdia guardian, security, someone who guards

waibi stream

waiddna heart

waiila need to, require, have to

wairshad factory

wairshad'o the factories

waihyll partner; mate; company

waihylli to accompany; accompany

wair to call (somebody) with mouth open

waisi ablution (*wudhu*)

waisi falo or **waisi qaazho** get ablution

waisi faliliy ablated

waizhd drive

waizhow driver

wal' stuff; thing

walaal sibling

wala stuff; thing

walag stir

walatzo something

wala kalle something else, another thing

walal a brother or a sister (depends on usage)

walaz sister

walba nothing, none

walbahrasho education

walid parent

walid diyn parent guardian

wallahi promise, swear

wallahi billahi tallahi Quttab Kee Jama the full swearing ritual, an oath to God (Allah)

walmaudhafow scavenger

walmauquure ungenerous, stingy

wal' mehe it's nothing, nothing

wana then, as well, also, and even

wanagsan well-founded, good

wani advice, guidance

waqti time

waqti kee the time, when

waqti wa it's time

waqti kaas that time

warab to drink

warabi to water (a garden or something)

warag paper

warag'o the papers

waranq spear

warar brother

warawo hyena

warawo kumbo monsters, wild hyenas

waraiji spin

waraijia *plural* spin

wareg to go around

waregso turn around or go around

wareg circle

wareg'o the circles

warer addle, confuse

wareri to make (someone) confused

wareriy past of *warer*

warmad menu

warqad paper letter

warrso ask

warr to ask

warroso to ask information, to interview

warroy to make (something or someone) a big deal

warroy to act all that

warya yo; hey you

wasacg dirty

wass fuck

wask sink

wask'o the sinks

waskan a twisted-mind person

waswas bad situation or condition, deep trouble, big problem

wa tou *feminine* right here

wauadi to preach

wauhh an expression of surprise, anger, excitement, etc.

waun these (used with nouns)

waurr rumor, situation

waurrey a person who spreads words or rumor around

wauc call out

wawarey an expression; "oh my gosh"

Way *plural* my

Waye are

wayail an old person that cannot do anything

wazeer chief executive office

Wazigula one of the Somali tribes that speaks Kizigula

wey an expression; "oh my god"

wee the (used when there is more than one)

weesh elevator

weeshrowg escalator

weinazhiy grew up

wein huge, large

weinai to make (something) grow, to enlarge

weinqo *masculine* huge, large *transitive verb*

weinto *feminine* huge, large *transitive verb*

weinaw grow up

weuell whoreson; baseborn

weyh where (used when it is about something or someone)

weyhkeyh to say where a male at

weyhkeyh usu where's he

weyhteyh *feminine* where

weyhteyh eeh where's she

weyr to make a sound, to call

weyri to make (something) to sound, to ring

weyriy past tense of *weyr*

weydi query, ask

weyl calf

whar an expression of anger; "look" or "just"

wranq chat, small talk, talk

wyllwyll worry

whydd to have on or to take (someone/something) with

whacg before sunrise

whel dish, food

whera surround attack

wiil boy

wiil athaig or **athaig wiil** errand boy

wiilsahib boyfriend

wiwio flamingo

wizhay a close friend, bestfriend

wo at time, some (used when there is more than one)

wochowocho speaker device

wouqti season

Wouqti kaas that season

wouji face

wua have to, need to

wujjo big mess of trouble

wyddi find, search

wyel do

wyeliy did

wylli still

wyrr to hang (cloth)

wyrriy past tense of *wairr*

wyyrshi ship

wyyshi modern, modern time

X

xaas wife

xai whoa, right?

xayaan insect

xyawaan *lexicon* "animal"

Y

yaab speechless, shock, stunned, astonished, heartbroken

yaal located, location (used when something in position), to say (something) on the ground or somewhere

yaalayena or **yaalang** *plural* were (here or there)

yaalayiy was (her or there)

yaalaytiy *feminine* was (here or there)

Yaqoob or **Yaqub** male name; role model; (American) Jacob

yahas aligator

yairi pronounce; call out; say out

yakke number one; one

yal *plural* (used for more than one)

yal kau your (used when the owned thing is plural)

yal kayno our (used when the owned thing is plural)

yal kay my (used when the owned thing is plural)

yal kee *plural* the (used in specific and certain stuff, things, or people)

yal kingh *plural* your (used when the owner is plural and the thing they own is plural)

yal sheh his, her, their (used for plural things)

yar young, little, less

yar a girl or a boy, a kid

yarai to make (something) small

yaris little, small, bit

yarow used to call an unknown boy, a young boy

yarey used to call an unknown girl, a young girl

yar kaas that boy

yar tzaas that girl

yas undervalue

yembo hoe, garden hoe

yembo wein pickax

yiriy *lexicon* said

yowbba already

yubb putting in or dipping

Yuhood Jewish

Yumbi or **dhimbi** sink

Yusuf male name; "God will increase"; (American) Joseph

yuub foreskin

yuuble a person that has foreskin

Z

zabb a party that is mainly for food

Zahara female name; flower

zahid too much, very

Zainab female name; beauty

zamaani ancient

zami tractor

zawib raisin

zeka benefaction, charity

Zeka first month

ziqle tomfool, bubblehead

Present Tense Table

Present Tense	Plural	Present Tense with "ing"	Plural (we) with "ing"	Plural (they) with "ing"
kouy: come	*kouya*	*kouyoye*: coming	*kouyoyne*	*kouyoyena/ kouyoyang*
ror: run	*Roar*	*roroye*: running	*roroyne*	*roroyena/ roroyang*
darrer: walk	*darrera*	*darreroye*: walking	*darreroyne*	*darreroyena/ darreroyang*
aanq: eat	*aama*	*aamoye*: eating	*aamoyne*	*aamoyena/ aamoyang*
bah: go	*baha*	*bahoye*: going	*bahoyne*	*bahoyena/ bahoyang*
rah: follow	*raha*	*rahoye*: following	*rahoyne*	*rahoyena/ rahoyang*
sheg: tell	*shega*	*shegoye*: telling	*shegoyne*	*shegoyena/ shegoyang*

Past Tense Table

Past tense	Feminine	Plural (we)	Plural (they)	Masculine
karriy: cooked	*karritiy*	*karriniy*	*karriang/karriena*	*karryiy*
kouyiy: came	*kouytiy*	*kouyniy*	*kouyang/kouyena*	*kouyiy*
roriy: ran	*rortiy*	*rorniy*	*rorang/rorena*	*roriy*
bahiy: left	*bahtiy*	*bahniy*	*bahang/bahena*	*bahiy*
darreriy: walked	*darrertiy*	*darrerniy*	*darrerang/ darrerena*	*darreriy*
aamiy: ate	*aanqtiy*	*aanqniy*	*aamang/aamena*	*aamiy*
ksheniy: brought	*kshenqtiy*	*kshenqniy*	*kshenang/kshenena*	*ksheniy*
rahiy: followed	*rahtiy*	*rahniy*	*rahang/rahena*	*rahiy*
shegiy: told	*shegtiy*	*shegniy*	*shegang/shegena*	*shegiy*

Genders

masculine *-kee* (the)
feminine *-tzee* (the)

Grammatical Genders for "Belongings"

(My)

kay, tzay

(Your)

kau, tzau

(His/Its)

sheh, kis, tzis

(Her)

sheh, kieh, tzieh

(Our)

kayno, tzayno

(Their)

sho

(plural)

Yal kay (my) */way*, yal *kau* (your) */wau*, yal *kayno* (our) */wayno*, *yal sheh* (his/her), *yal kis* (his), *yal kieh* (her), *yal sho* (their)

Belonging Words for "My" Usage

My name ...	*Maga kay ...*
My father ...	*Aaw kay ...*
My young sister ...	*Walaz tzay ...*
My grandfather ...	*Awoa kay ...*
My wife ...	*Xaas tzay ...*
My thing ...	*wala kay ...*
My siblings ...	*Walaal yal kay ...*
It is mine ...	*Kee kay wa ...*

Belonging (Old Female Relative) Words for "My" Usage

My mother ...	*Aay tzay ...*
My grandmother ...	*Awoy tzay ...*
My elder-sister ...	*Abay tzay ...*
My mama ...	*Mama tzay ...*
My aunty ...	*Innay tzay ...*
My stepmother ...	*Aido tzay ...*
It is mine ...	*Tzee tzay wa ...*

Belonging Words for "Your" Usage

Your young sister ...	*Walaz tzau ...*
Your house ...	*Minink kau ...*
Your wife ...	*Xaas tzau ...*
Your elder brother ...	*Abou kau ...*
Your siblings ...	*Walaal yal kau ...*
Your hand ...	*Gauan tzau ...*
Your name ...	*Maga kau ...*
It is yours ...	*Kee kau wa ...*

Belonging (Old Female Relative) Words for "Your" Usage

Your mother …	*Aay tzau* …
Your grandmother …	*Awoy tzau* …
Your elder-sister …	*Abay tzau* …
Your mama …	*Mama tzau* …
Your aunty …	*Innay tzau* …
Your stepmother …	*Aido tzau* …
It is yours …	*Tzee tzau wa* …

Belonging Words for "Our" Usage

Our name …	*Maga kayno* …
Our elder-brother …	*Abou kayno* …
Our uncle …	*Apti kayno* …
Our house …	*Minink kayno* …
Our thing …	*Wala kayno* …
Our children …	*Ilm yal kayno* …
Our young sister …	*Walaz tzayno* …
It is ours …	*Kee kayno wa* …

Belonging (Old Female Relative) Words for "Our" Usage

Our mother …	*Aay tzayno* …
Our grandmother …	*Awoy tzayno* …
Our elder-sister …	*Abay tzayno* …
Our mama …	*Mama tzayno* …
Our aunty …	*Innay tzayno* …
Our stepmother …	*Aido tzayno* …
It is ours …	*Tzee tzayno wa* …

Belonging Words for "His/Its" Usage

His T-shirt ...	Shati sheh ...
His shoes ...	Kobb yal sheh ...
His elder brother ...	Abou sheh ...
His hands ...	Gauan yal sheh ...
His young sister ...	Walaz tzis ...
His thing ...	Wala sheh ...
His uncle ...	Apti sheh ...
It is his or its ...	Kee sheh wa ...

Belonging (Old Female Relative) Words for "His" Usage

His mother ...	Aay tzis ...
His grandmother ...	Awoy tzis ...
His elder-sister ...	Abay tzis ...
His mama ...	Mama tzis ...
His aunty ...	Innay tzis ...
His stepmother ...	Aido tzis ...
It is his ...	Tzee tzis wa ...

Belonging Words for "Her" Usage

Her papa ...	Baba sheh ...
Her young sister ...	walaz tzieh ...
Her nephew ...	Aisinq sheh ...
Her niece ...	Aisin sheh ...
Her nose ...	Sanq sheh ...
Her elder brother ...	Abou sheh ...
Her door ...	Ilbab sheh ...
It is hers ...	Kee sheh wa ...

Belonging (Old Female Relative) Words for "Her" Usage

Her mother ...	*Aay tzieh* ...
Her grandmother ...	*Awoy tzieh* ...
Her elder-sister ...	*Abay tzieh* ...
Her mama ...	*Mama tzieh* ...
Her aunty ...	*Innay tzieh* ...
Her stepmother ...	*Aido tzieh* ...
It is hers ...	*Tzee tzieh wa* ...

Belonging Words for "Their" Usage

Their girl ...	*Gaiwyrr sho* ...
Their boy ...	*Inanq sho* ...
Their father ...	*Aaw sho* ...
Their elder-brother ...	*Abou sho* ...
Their house ...	*Minink sho* ...
Their grandfather ...	*Awoa sho* ...
Their young sister ...	*Walaz tzhio* ...
It is theirs ...	*Kee sho wa* ...

Belonging (Old Female Relative) Words for "Their" Usage

Their mother ...	*Aay tzio* ...
Their grandmother ...	*Awoy tzio* ...
Their elder-sister ...	*Abay tzio* ...
Their mama ...	*Mama tzio* ...
Their aunty ...	*Innay tzio* ...
Their stepmother ...	*Aido tzio* ...
It is theirs ...	*Tzee tzio wa* ...

Plural Tables

Belonging Words for "Your" Usage

Your name ...	*Maga kingh ...*
Your boy ...	*Inanq kingh ...*
Your house ...	*Minink kingh ...*
Your grandmother ...	*Awoy tzingh ...*
Your mother ...	*Harti kingh ...*
Your grandfather ...	*Awoa kingh ...*
Your water ...	*Biyo kingh ...*
It is yours ...	*Kee kingh wa ...*

Belonging (Old Female Relative) Words for "Your" Usage

Your mother ...	*Aay tzingh ...*
Your grandmother ...	*Awoy tzingh ...*
Your elder-sister ...	*Abay tzingh ...*
Your mama ...	*Mama tzingh ...*
Your aunty ...	*Innay tzingh ...*
Your stepmother ...	*Aido tzingh ...*
It is yours ...	*Tzee tzingh wa ...*

Belonging Words for "Your" Usage

Your shoes ...	*Kobb yal kau ...*
Your cheeks ...	*khanq yal kau ...*
Your boobytraps ...	*Uayy yal kau ...*
Your dogs ...	*Ey yal kau ...*
Your logs ...	*Kurdtunq yal kau ...*
Your cockroaches ...	*Barambara yal kau ...*
Your rockets ...	*Meeg yal kau ...*
They are yours ...	*Kwee wau wa ...* or *kwee yal kau wa ...*

Belonging (Old Female Relative) Words for "Your" Usage

Your mothers ...	*Aay yal kau ...*
Your grandmothers ...	*Awoy yal kau ...*
Your elder-sisters ...	*Abay yal kau ...*
Your mamas ...	*Mama yal kau ...*
Your aunts ...	*Innay yal kau ...*
Your stepmothers ...	*Aido yal kau ...*
They are yours ...	*Kwee nau wa ...*

Belonging for "Your" Usage

Your names ...	*Maga yal kingh ...*
Your sons ...	*Inanq yal kingh ...*
Your mothers ...	*Aay yal kingh ...*
Your aunts ...	*Innay yal kingh ...*
Your fathers ...	*Aaw yal kingh ...*
Your elder-sisters ...	*Abay yal kingh ...*
Your elder-brothers ...	*Abou yal kingh ...*
They are yours ...	*Kwee ningh wa ...*

Belonging (Old Female Relative and Plural) Words for "Your" Usage

Your mothers ...	*Aay yal kingh ...*
Your grandmothers ...	*Awoy yal kingh ...*
Your elder-sisters ...	*Abay yal kingh ...*
Your mamas ...	*Mama yal kingh ...*
Your aunts ...	*Innay yal kingh ...*
Your stepmothers ...	*Aido yal kingh ...*
They are yours ...	*Kwee ningh wa ...*

Belonging Words for "Our" Usage

Our fathers ...	*Aaw yal kayno ...*
Our houses ...	*Minink yal kayno ...*
Our children ...	*Ilm yal kayno ...*
Our uncles ...	*Apti yal kayno ...*
Our axes ...	*Missar yal kayno ...*
Our doors ...	*Ilbab yal kayno ...*
Our telephones ...	*Taar yal kayno ...*
They are ours ...	*Kwee kayno wa ...* or *kwee yal kayno wa ...*

Belonging (Old Female Relative) Words for "Our" Usage

Our mothers ...	*Aay yal kayno ...*
Our grandmothers ...	*Awoy yal kayno ...*
Our elder-sisters ...	*Abay yal kayno ...*
Our mamas ...	*Mama yal kayno ...*
Our aunts ...	*Innay yal kayno ...*
Our stepmothers ...	*Aido yal kayno ...*
They are ours ...	*Kwee tzayno way' ...*

Belonging Words for "My" Usage

My stepfathers ...	*Athair yal kay ...*
My uncles ...	*Apti yal kay ...*
My children ...	*Ilm yal kay ...*
My hands ...	*Gauan yal kay ...*
My boys ...	*Inanq yal kay ...*
My girls ...	*Gaiwyrr yal kay ...*
My fingers ...	*Farr yal kay ...*
They are mine ...	*Kwee kay way' ...*

Belonging (Old Female Relative) Words for "My" Usage

My mothers ...	*Aay yal kay* ...
My grandmothers ...	*Awoy yal kay* ...
My elder-sisters ...	*Abay yal kay* ...
My mamas ...	*Mama yal kay* ...
My aunts ...	*Innay yal kay* ...
My stepmothers ...	*Aido yal kay* ...
They are mine ...	*Kwee tzay way'* ... or *kwee yal kay way'* ...

Belonging Words for "His" Usage

His women ...	*Naag yal sheh* ...
His people ...	*Daidd yal sheh* ...
His forests ...	*Duur yal sheh* ...
His onions ...	*Bassal yal sheh* ...
His pigs ...	*Donqfaar yal sheh* ...
His exits ...	*Irrid yal sheh* ...
His donkeys ...	*Damer yal sheh* ...
They are his ...	*Kwee sheh way'* ...

Belonging (Old Female Relative) Words for "His" Usage

His mothers ...	*Aay yal sheh* ...
His grandmothers ...	*Awoy yal sheh* ...
His elder-sisters ...	*Abay yal sheh* ...
His mamas ...	*Mama yal sheh* ...
His aunts ...	*Innay yal sheh* ...
His stepmothers ...	*Aido yal sheh* ...
They are his ...	*Kwee sheh way'* ... or *kwee yal sheh way'* ...

Belonging for "Their" Usage

Their children …	*Ilmo sho* …
Their girls …	*Gaiwyrr yal sho* …
Their children …	*Ilm yal sho* …
Their bikes …	*Baskiil yal sho* …
Their booby traps …	*Uayy yal sho* …
Their fathers …	*Aaw yal sho* …
Their husbands …	*Harti yal sho* …
They are theirs …	*Kwee sho way'* …

Belonging (Old Female Relative) Words for "Their" Usage

Their mothers …	*Aay yal sho* …
Their grandmothers …	*Awoy yal sho* …
Their elder-sisters …	*Abay yal sho* …
Their mamas …	*Mama yal sho* …
Their aunts …	*Innay yal sho* …
Their stepmothers …	*Aido yal sho* …
They are theirs …	*Kwee tzio way'* … or *kwee yal sho way'* …

Main Implication/Variant Words

ei implies "me"

ki" implies "you"

ni implies "us"

si or *sin* implies "you guys"

Did

Euy? Did?

Examples:

He: *Usu ror euy?* Did he run?

I: *Ani ror euy?* Did I run?

You: *Athi rort euy?* Did you run?

She: *Eeh rort euy?* Did she run?

We: *Unu rorn euy?* Did we run?

Euyna? Did? (used with "you guys", "they" and "people")

Examples:

You guys: *Ising kouyt euyna?* Did you guys come?

They: *Eeyo kouy euyna?* Did they come?

People: *Daidd kee kouy euyna?* Did the people come?

English to Mai-Mai Phrases

Did/Eat

Did you eat? *Athi aanqt euy?*—Yes, I ate! *Haa, ani aamiy!*

Did he eat? *Usu aam euy?*—Yes, he ate! *Haa, usu aamiy!*

Did she eat? *Eeh aanqt euy?*—Yes, she ate! *Haa, eeh aanqtiy!*

Did they eat? *Eeyo aam euyna?*—Yes, they ate! *Haa, eeyo aamena/aamang!*

Did we eat? *Unu aanqn euy?*—Yes, you guys ate! *Haa, ising aanqtena/aanqtang!*

Did I eat? *Ani aam euy?*—Yes, you ate! *Haa, athi aanqtiy!*

Did you guys eat? *Ising aanqt euyna?*—Yes, we ate! *Haa, unu aanqniy!*

Did/Bring

Did you bring bread? *Routi athi kshenqt euy?*—No, I did not bring bread! *Mayya, routi ani mau kshen nea!*

Did he bring bread? *Routi usu kshen euy?*—No, he did not bring bread! *Mayya, routi usu mau kshen nea!*

Did she bring bread? *Routi eeh kshenqt euy?*—No, she did not bring bread! *Mayya, routi eeh mau kshen nea!*

Did I bring bread? *Routi ani kshen euy?*—No, you did not bring bread! *Mayya, routi athi mau kshen nea!*

Did we bring bread? *Routi unu kshenqn euy?*—No, you guys did not bring bread! *Mayya, routi ising mau kshen nea!*

Did they bring bread? *Routi eeyo kshen euyna?*—No, they did not bring bread! *Mayya, routi eeyo mau kshen nea!*

Did you guys bring bread? *Routi ising kshenqt euyna?*—No, we did not bring bread! *Mayya, routi unu mau kshen nea!*

Will/Bring

Will you guys bring eggs? *Ising kshenas aihna ukun yal?*—No, we will not bring eggs! *Mayya, unu mau kshenano ukun yal!*

Will they bring eggs? *Eeyo kshena aihna ukun yal?*—No, they will not bring eggs! *Mayya, eeyo mau kshenaona ukun yal!*

Will we bring eggs? *Unu kshenan aih ukun yal?*—No, you guys will not bring eggs! *Mayya, ising mau kshenasona ukun yal!*

Will I bring eggs? *Ani kshen aih ukun yal?*—No, you will not bring eggs! *Mayya, athi mau kshenaso ukun yal!*

Will she bring eggs? *Eeh kshenas aih ukun yal?*—No, she will not bring eggs! *Mayya, eeh mau kshenaso ukun yal!*

Will he bring eggs? *Usu kshen aih ukun yal?*—No, he will not bring eggs! *Mayya, usu mau kshenaw ukun yal!*

Will you bring eggs? *Athi kshenas aih ukun yal?*—No, I will not bring eggs! *Mayya, ani mau kshenaw ukun yal!*

What/Want

What do you want? *Mai athi rawbte?*—I want my son! *Ani inanq kay rawe!*

What does she want? *Mai eeh rawbte?*—She wants her son! *Eeh inanq sheh rawbte!*

What does he want? *Mai usu rawe?*—He wants his son! *Usu inanq sheh rawe!*

What do they want? *Mai eeyo rawena?*—They want their son! *Eeyo inanq sho rawena/rawang!*

What do you guys want? *Mai ising rawbtena?*—We want our son! *Unu inanq kayno rawbne!*

Go

You go! *Athi bah!*

You guys go! *Ising baha!*

You guys all go! *Ising kulli baha!*

All of you go! *Ising kulli kingh baha!*

Leave

Leave her! *Dhaf eeh!*

Leave him! *Dhaf usu!*

Leave me! *Ei dhaf!*

Leave them! *Dhaf eeyo!*

Leave us! *Ni dhaf!*

Name

My name? Maga kay?

My names? Maga yal kay?

Her name? *Maga kieh?*

Her names? *Maga yal kieh?*

His name? *Maga kis?*

His names? *Maga yal kis?*

Their name? *Maga sho?*

Their names? *Maga yal sho?*

Your name? *Maga kau?*

Your names? *Maga yal kau?*

You guys' names? *Ising maga yal kingh?*

What/Name

What is your name? *Mai wa maga kau?*

What is his name? *Mai wa maga sheh?* Or *mai wa usu maga sheh?*

What is her name? *Mai wa maga sheh?* Or *mai wa eeh maga sheh?*

What are their names? *Mai wa maga sho?*

What are your names? *Mai wa maga yal kau?*

What

What is she? *Mai wa eeh?*

What is he? *Mai wa usu?*

What are they? *Mai way' eeyo?*

What are we? *Mai way' unu?*

What are you? *Mai atte athi?*

What are you guys? *Mai way' ising?*

Who

Who is it? *Uai wa?*

Who are you? *Uai atte athi?*

who are you guys? *Uai attena ising?*

Who is this? *Uai wa kaun?*

Who is that? *Uai wa kaas?*

Who is he? *Uai wa usu?*

Who is she? *Uai wa eeh?*

Who are they? *Uai ayyena eeyo?*

Who am I? *Uai ayye ani?*

Running

I'm running! *Ani roroye!*

He's running! *Usu roroye!*

She's running! *Eeh roroyte!*

We're running! *Unu roroyne!*

You guys're running! *Ising roroytena!*

They're running! *Eeyo roroyang/roroyena!*

Was/Were Running

I was running! *Ani rorayiy!*

He was running! *Usu rorayiy!*

You were running! *Athi roraytiy!*

She was running! *Eeh roraytiy!*

We were running! *Unu rorayniy!*

They were running! *Eeyo rorayena/rorayang!*

You guys were running! *Ising roraytena/roraytang!*

Smoke

Do you smoke? *Athi dhoogase?*—No, I don't smoke! *Mayya, ani mau dhoogaw!*

Do they smoke? *Eeyo dhoogaena?*—No, they don't smoke! *Mayya, eeyo mau dhoogaona!*

Does she smoke? *Eeh dhoogase?*—No, she doesn't smoke! *Mayya, eeh mau dhoogaso!*

Does he smoke? *Usu dhooge?*—No, he doesn't smoke! *Mayya, usu mau dhoogaw!*

Do you guys smoke? *Ising dhoogasena?*—No, we don't smoke! *Mayya, unu mau dhoogano!*

Smoking

I am smoking cigarette! *Ani dhoogoye sigar!*

He is smoking cigarette! *Usu dhoogoye sigar!*

She is smoking cigarette! *Eeh dhoogoyte sigar!*

We are smoking cigarette! *Unu dhoogoyne sigar!*

You are smoking cigarette! *Athi dhoogoyte sigar!*

They are smoking cigarette! *Eeyo dhoogoyena/dhoogoyang sigar!*

You guys are smoking cigarette! *Ising dhoogoytena/dhoogoytang sigar!*

Was/Were Smoking

I was smoking! *Ani dhoogayiy!*

He was smoking! *Usu dhoogayiy!*

You were smoking! *Athi dhoogaytiy!*

She was smoking! *Eeh dhoogaytiy!*

We were smoking! *Unu dhoogayniy!*

They were smoking! *Eeyo dhoogayena/dhoogayang!*

You guys were smoking! *Ising dhoogaytena/dhoogaytang!*

When Will

When will she go? *Uama eeh bahas aih?*

When will I bring it? *Uama ani kshen aih?*

When will he come? *Uama usu kouy aih?*

When will you come? *Uama athi kouyas aih?*

When will she come? *Uama eeh kouyas aih?*

When will you bring it? *Uama athi kshenas aih?*

When will they come? *Uama eeyo kouya aihna?*

When will they bring it? *Uama eeyo kshena aihna?*

When will you guys fix this? *Uama ising soobias aihna kaun?*

Will Come

I will come! *Ani kouy aih!*

He will come! *Usu kouy aih!*

We will come! *Unu kouyan aih!*

You will come! *Athi kouyas aih!*

She will come! *Eeh kouyas aih!*

You guys will come! *Ising kouyas aihna!*

They will come! *Eeyo kouya aihna!*

Will Run

You will run! *Athi roras aih!*

You guys will run! *Ising roras aihna!*

We will run! *Unu roran aih!*

I will run! *Ani ror aih!*

She will run! *Eeh roras aih!*

He will run! *Usu ror aih!*

They will run! *Eeyo rora aihna!*

Don't

I don't want it! *Ani mau rawo!*

He doesn't want it! *Usu mau rawo!*

We don't want it! *Unu mau rawbno!*

She doesn't want it! *Eeh mau rawbto!*

I don't want him! *Ani mau rawo usu!*

I don't want that! *Ani mau rawo kaas!*

He doesn't want her! *Usu mau rawo eeh!*

She doesn't want this! *Eeh mau rawbto kaun!*

He doesn't want children! *Usu mau rawo ilm yal!*

They don't want it! *Eeyo mau rawang/rawona!*

You guys don't want it! *Ising mau rawbtona/rawbtang!*

She doesn't want that boy! *Eeh mau rawbto inanq kaas!*

Picture

Take picture of me! *Masewyr o qazhd/uss ani!* Or *ei masewyr!*

Take picture of us! *Masewyr no qazhd unu!* Or *ni masewyr!*

Take picture of them! *Masewyr ka qazhd eeyo!* Or *eeyo masewyr!*

Take picture of him! *Masewyr ka qazhd usu!* Or *usu masewyr!*

Take picture of her! *Masewyr ka qazhd eeh!* Or *eeh masewyr!*

Take picture of all of them! *Masewyr ka qazhd eeyo kulli!* Or *eeyo kulli masewyr!*

Happened

What happened? *Mai dhyiy?*

What happened here? *Mai dhyiy inti?*

What happened to them? *Mai ka dhyiy eeyo?*

What happened to her? *Mai ka dhyiy eeh?*

What happened to him? *Mai ka dhyiy usu?*

What happened to me? *Mai o dhyiy ani?*

What happened to you? *Mai ko dhyiy athi?*

What happened to us? *Mai no dhyiy unu?*

What happened to you guys? *Mai ising sin ka dhyiy?*

Luck

He has luck! *Usu nasib kawe!*

I have luck! *Ani nasib kawe!*

We have luck! *Unu nasib kawbne!*

You have luck! *Athi nasib kawbte!*

She has luck! *Eeh nasib kawbte!*

They have luck! *Eeyo nasib kawang/kawena!*

You guys have luck! *Ising nasib kawbtena/kawbtang!*

Miss

You miss me! *Athi in hilowtiy ani!*

I miss you! *Ani ki in hilowiy athi!*

She misses me! *Eeh in hilowtiy ani!*

He misses me! *Usu in hilowiy ani!*

She misses us! *Eeh ni in hilowtiy unu!*

We miss you guys! *Unu si in hilowniy ising!*

Your mother misses us! *Aay tzau ni in hilowtiy unu!*

You guys miss me! *Ising in hilowtena ani!*

You guys miss your uncle! *Ising in hilowtena apti kingh!*

She misses you! *Eeh ki in hilowtiy athi!*

Your aunt misses you! *Innay tzau ki in hilowtiy athi!*

They miss you! *Eeyo ki in hilowena/hilowang athi!*

Your elder brothers miss you! *Abou yal kau ki in hilowena/hilowang Athi!*

I miss you guys! *Ani si in hilowiy ising!*

I miss your elder sister! *Ani in hilowiy abay tzau!* Or *abay tzau in hillowiy!*

We miss you! *Unu ki in hilowniy athi!* Or *ki in hilowniy!*

Why don't/can't you eat…?

Why don't you eat it? *Mai athi aanqt i usu?* Or *Mai athi is ka aanqt i?*

Why you can't eat them? *Mai athi in aanq waaysinte eeyo?* Or *Mai athi is ka aanq waaysinte?*

Why you cannot eat him? *Mai athi mau in aanq qarto usu?* Or *Mai athi mau in aanq qarto?*

Why don't/can't he make…?

Why don't he make a house? *Mai usu sameay i minink?* Or *Mai usu minink is ka sameay i?*

Why he cannot make a house? *Mai usu mau in sameay qaro minink?*

Why he can't make houses? *Mai usu in sameay waaysinye minink yal?* Or *Mai usu is ka sameay waaysinye minink yal?*

Conversations

Hello ... *Haye* ...

How are you? *Seithyy atte athi?*—I'm fine! *Ani faye!*

How is your family? *Seithyy ayyena/ayyang Famil kau!*—They are fine! *Eeyo fayena/fayang!*

Where are you going? *Inteyh athi in bahoyte?*—I'm going to the mall! *Ani in bahoye soog tzee!*

Okay, we will see each other some other time! *Hayye, unu is aragan aih marr quo kalle!*

Seasons in Mai-Mai

jilal - summer

dhi - fall

goo - winter

aaran - spring

Days of the Week in Mai-Mai

Asneen - Monday

Talaatha - Tuesday

Arbah - Wednesday

Khamees - Thursday

Jummah - Friday

Saibti - Saturday

Ahad - Sunday

Colors (*Noaua yal*)

red - *gazhud*

orange - *bazhul*

green - *agaar*

purple - *kaibaidd*

scarlet - *asan*

yellow - *jaale*

gray - *pimbais*

black - *mazhow*

pink - *blubb*

blue - *buloog*

brown - *dhule*

Islamic Months in Mai-Mai

Zeka - January (*Muharram*)

Safar - February (*Safar*)

Mowlid - March (*Rabi al-Awwal*)

Maalmadon - April (*Rabi al-Thani*)

Meyleehore - May (*Jumada al-awwal*)

Meyleedambe - June (*Jumada al-Thani*)

Auw Usman - July (*Rajab*)

Shauaban - August (*Shaaban*)

Songh - September (*Ramadan*)

Songhfurr - October (*Shawwal*)

Sieaital - November (*Dhu'l-Qadah*)

Arafah - December (*Dhu'l-Hijja*)

CPSIA information can be obtained
at www.ICGtesting.com
Printed in the USA
BVHW030949180619
551304BV00002B/305/P